THE THEATRICAL WRITINGS OF
Fabrizio Carini Motta

TRANSLATIONS OF

Trattato sopra la struttura de'Theatri e scene, 1676

AND

Costruzione de teatri e machine teatrali, 1688

With an Introduction by

ORVILLE K. LARSON

Southern Illinois University Press · Carbondale and Edwardsville

Edited by Teresa White

Designed by David Ford

Production supervised by Natalia Nadraga

Library of Congress Cataloging-in-Publication Data

Carini Motta, Fabricio.
    The theatrical writings of Fabrizio Carini Motta.
    Includes index.
    1. Theaters—Italy—Construction.   2. Architecture,
Baroque—Italy.   I. Larson, Orville K. (Orville
Kurth), 1914–.   II. Carini Motta, Fabricio.
Costruzione de teatri e machine teatrali. English.
1987.   III. Title.
NA6840.I7C2713   1987   725′.822′0945   87–4296
ISBN 0–8093–1337–5

Stephano bella Della. Scene from *La Garaddle Stagione,* Ferrara, 1652.
The Metropolitan Museum of Art, The Elisha Whittelsey Collection, The Elisha
Whittelsey Fund, 1967. (67.542.6)

For Helen

Contents

Acknowledgments

Acknowledgments must begin with the recognition of the influence of three teachers whose academic standards became a constant guide and whose intellectual integrity an enduring goal; namely those eminent architectural historians Turpin Bannister and Alain Lang, who first introduced me to the joys of pure research, and that philosopher of theatre history, George Kernodle, whose influence goes back to those Saturday afternoons when we sat in the Library of the Cleveland Museum of Art where he expounded his theories "From Art to Theatre" long before the manuscript found its way into print. George Kernodle turned my interest in the Italian theatre into a lifelong pursuit. Through the years these men became more than mentors, they became lifelong friends.

Relative to the Motta research I am indebted to the Comune di Modena and Dr. Ernesto Milano, Director of the Biblioteca Estense in Modena, Italy, for making the *Construzione* manuscript available and granting permission to publish its plates. I am grateful to Dr. Gian Carlo Schizzerotto, Director of the Biblioteca Communale in Mantova, Italy, for the help of his generous staff, and most of all to Dr. Adelle Bellú, Director of the Archivio di Stato in Mantova, who for several years not only answered all my inquiries about Carini Motta and the Gonzaga court with dispatch but who also ferreted out bits of relevant information unsolicited. I shall long remember her courtesies.

I thank the Print Department of the Metropolitan Museum of Art for permission to reproduce Stephano della Bella's etching of the theatre in Ferrara, the Archivio di Stato in Mantova for permission to reproduce the floor plan of Motta's remodeled Teatro dei Comici and the Biblioteca Communale of Mantova for permission to reproduce the etching of Carini Motta's cloud machines.

Of all of those who have assisted in my research on Carini Motta over the past decade none have been more helpful than C. Thomas Ault who provided yeoman service in deciphering that fine Italian hand of the eighteenth-century copyist for the initial draft of the *Costruzione* translation. He has my profound gratitude for his enthusiasm and help.

Acknowledgments

A grant from the American Philosophical Society made an Italian trip possible in 1983, and I am also beholden to the Office of Research and Sponsored Programs of Kent State University for a Research Fellowship in 1978 as well as several other travel grants.

I wish to acknowledge the editorial assistance of Teresa White of the Southern Illinois University Press. Her enthusiasm for a subject as involved as the *Costruzione* is refreshing indeed.

And finally, I am grateful for the help and encouragement of my wife Helen who marshaled the Motta studies through several drafts and revisions. Her cheerful enthusiasm in putting up with my scholastic idiosyncrasies—as the work took its present form—has made the mechanics of preparation seem almost nonexistent. It is to her this work is dedicated.

A Note on the Translations

When the Italians modernized the spelling and punctuation in the text of the reprint edition of the *Trattato* in 1972 Edward A. Craig, who had persuaded them to publish the reprint, felt so strongly about the changes that he published a photostat of the original a decade later, justifying his action with the inquiry, "Who wants to study Vasari from a translation?" As Stark Young once pointed out, translating is a hazardous business, for the translator never satisfies everyone. Literalists like Craig expect exact translations, while others less demanding are satisfied with contemporary transcriptions.

The problem certainly exists in translating the *Trattato* and especially the *Costruzione,* for in both there are obsolete terms that need modernizing and others—like the term *gargamo*—whose meaning must be adapted to each explanation, as they are terms the Italians used to classify different objects that have a similar use.

Thus, the translations of the *Trattato* and the *Costruzione* are not literal, word-for-word philologically correct translations. We have tried instead to produce texts that are simple, clear, and readable for the theatre buff as well as the specialist, yet keeping both the spirit and tone of the original. A certain amount of interpretation was necessary inasmuch as what Carini Motta occasionally omits is just as important as what he records, requiring the translator to bring a keen understanding of the objects and methods being explained. This is particularly true regarding the plates of machinery.

That Fabrizio Carini Motta was a facile stage machinist as well as an opinionated theatre architect is evident throughout his writings. We are grateful that he kept his promise—at the end of the *Trattato*—to write another book, for the *Costruzione* is a unique source of seventeenth-century Italian stagecraft heretofore unexplained, as the present translation makes clear.

THE THEATRICAL WRITINGS OF
Fabrizio Carini Motta

Introduction

The theatre architect/scene designer/stage machinist Fabrizio Carini Motta (1627–99) is the author of *Trattato sopra la struttura de' Theatri e scene* (Treatise on the structure of theatres and scenes), published in Guastella, Italy, in 1676 and *Costruzione de' teatri e machine teatrali* (Construction of theatres and theatrical machinery), an unpublished manuscript dated 1688. The work of Fabrizio Carini Motta is unknown to most theatre historians, and it is our hope that with the publication of the translations of his theatrical writings (the first of several studies planned about Motta's theatrical activities), Carini Motta's importance will emerge and the value of his writings will be recognized for what they are: primary source material—firsthand observations and opinions about seventeenth-century Italian theatre architecture and stagecraft by a practicing theatre artist.

Fabrizio Carini Motta

Fabrizio Carini Motta served the Gonzaga court in Mantova, Italy, as Prefect of Theatres and Architect to the Duke Ferdinando Carlo IV between 1671 and 1699, the waning years of the Gonzaga dynasty. Although records indicate that Carini Motta was born in Mantova, the son of the public notary Nicola Motta in 1627,[1] there is little information about his life and activities before his appointment to the court besides the fact that he was educated as a painter.[2]

Carini Motta began working officially in the Gonzaga court in 1671 when Duke Carlo IV appointed him "Superintendent of Buildings and Prefect of Theatres."[3] The codicil to a will reveals that by 1669 Motta had built a theatre for a Mantovan citizen named Luigi Fedeli, but little is known about this theatre except that it was a public playhouse.[4] By 1673 Motta was promi-

[1] Archivio di Stato, Mantova, Italy, *Documenti Parti D'Arco N225. Mille scrittori Mantova (sec. XIV–XIX), notize delle accademie dei giornali e delle typographie, che furono in Mantova*, Vol. II BEL-CAPHI, n.d.

[2] Duke Carlo IV mentions this fact in his proclamation of 1699. See n. 9.

[3] *Archivio Gonzaga, registro patenti*, libro 13, c 151 t, 9 luglio 1671.

[4] *Archivio Gonzaga*, busta H VIII, 3–6.

nently engaged in court theatricals as architect and scene designer and two years later he was promoted to "Architect to the Duke," a position he held for the rest of his life.[5] As court architect, he provided elaborate catafalques for royal funerals.[6] Motta published the *Trattato* in 1676 and he left in manuscript the unpublished *Costruzione,* dated 1688, the same year he was commissioned to renovate the eighty-year-old Teatro dei Comici.[7] The registry of court dependents still listed him as court architect in 1697 at the age of seventy.[8] Two years later he was lauded by the duke for his lifetime service in a royal proclamation that states, "for his various and continuous substantial service to Our House for a continued period of fifty years, particularly as a painter to His Highness Duke Carlo IV, Our Lord and Master, whereas he actually worked as superintendent of theatres and architecture, with his great talent so conspicuous on so many occasions. We wish him to enjoy during his natural life all the benefits, salaries and privileges which he has up to now enjoyed."[9]

Duke Carlo's remarks about Motta's continuous service are obviously erroneous, since Motta began his official service in 1671, indicating twenty-eight rather than fifty years of service. Apparently in his accolade to Carini Motta, the duke included in his thinking the services of another Motta, Giovanni Francesco Motta, who served as Prefect of Theatres and Architect to the Gonzaga court between 1642 and 1654. The error is responsible for the mistaken belief that Carini Motta's services to the Gonzaga court began in 1649.[10]

Official functions of a theatrical nature during Duke Carlo IV's tenure were few because the duke's political activities kept him out of Mantova for long periods of time. One was an elaborate festival of fireworks celebrating the election of Pope Clement X in 1670 and another was the *Festa di Mantua*

[5] *Archivio Gonzaga, registro patenti,* libro 13, c 9, doc., 19 febbraio 1675.

[6] See *Le esequie celebratesi nella chiesa si S. Orsola in Mantova d'ordine del. Arcid. Isabella Clara duchessa di Mantova per la morte della Imp. Aug. Claudia Felice di lei nipote* (Mantova, 1675) and *Le esequie celebratesi nella chiesa Ducale di S. Barbaradi comando del Sr. Sig. Duca Ferdinando Carlo, Duca di Mantova, Monferrato e Guastella per la morte della Seren. Signora Arciduchessa Maria di Lui madre* (Mantova, 1685) for detailed descriptions of Carini Motta's "apparato funbre."

[7] Among the notes of Stephano Davari, nineteenth-century historian of Mantovan theatrical activities, *Archivio Gonzaga,* H VIII, busta 14.

[8] *Archivio Gonzaga,* busta 396 (1697).

[9] *Archivio Gonzaga, registro mandati,* libro 61, 9 aprile, 1699.

[10] See Edward A. Craig's introduction to the 1972 reprint edition of the *Trattato.* A few years later, Adriano Cavicchi, commenting on Motta's unpublished *Costruzione,* repeats Craig's initial errors. See Cavicchi, "Scenotecnica e Macchinistica Teatrale in un Trattato inedito di Fabrizio Carini Motta" (Mantova, 1688), in Maria Teresa Muraro, *Venezia e il Melodramma nel Seicento* (Firenze, 1976) 359–77.

in 1673. To celebrate the opening of the renovated Teatro dei Comici in 1688, the duke and his wife entertained the citizens of Mantova with an elaborate mask ball and equestrian show. The funeral ceremonies of the archduchess Claudia Felice in 1675, Maria Gonzaga in 1685, Elenora Gonzaga, the empress of Austria in 1687, and Leonora Maria Gioseffa, archduchess of Austria in 1698 all assumed characteristics of court celebrations.

Although public performances of traveling Commedia troupes appeared continuously at the Teatro delle Commedie and the Teatro dei Comici during Motta's lifetime, the Gonzaga court saw only twelve legitimate theatrical productions—i.e., dramas, dramas "with music," tragedies, and *pastorales* between 1672 and 1699. Although Carini Motta is identified specifically with only two, we believe that in his official capacity as prefect of theatres he was associated with all the court productions as well as those occurring in the public playhouses.[11]

Duke Carlo IV was an avid fan of Venetian opera who spent as much time in Venice as he did in Mantova. The duke was a notorious figure in Venetian society who during carnival seasons entertained often in his Venetian palazzo.[12] Carini Motta quite likely joined the duke's retinue frequently, for it is obvious from Motta's statements (as well as others) that Carini Motta was as well informed about the theatre architecture of the Venetian opera houses and the techniques of the Venetian stage machinists as he was of the forms and practices of the older court theatres in the Emilia-Romagna and the Veneto regions of northern Italy. Motta states at one point in the *Trattato*, "I have seen many theatres."

In addition to the theatres in Mantova and its surrounding villas, we believe that Carini Motta was familiar with the Teatro Olympico in Sabbionetta, the Teatro Salone (Farnese), and the Teatro Raccetta in Parma, the Teatro Ruggeri in Guastella, the Teatro Vecchio in Carpi, the Teatro Obizzi in Ferrara, and the Teatro della Spelta in Modena, as well as several playhouses in Venice. Others in Bologna, Florence, and Rome he probably had less opportunity to see.[13] However, Carini Motta's subtitle to the *Trattato* states that he is discussing methodology "as in our times is customary, ac-

[11] For a résumé of these activities, see Emilio Faccioli, *Mantova Le Lettre,* Vol. III (Milano, 1963), and Giuseppe Amadei *I 150 anni dei sociale storia dei Teatri di Mantova* (Mantova, 1973).

[12] For one account of Duke Carlo's social activities in Venice, see A. T. Limojon de St. Dider, *The City and the Republic of Venice* (London), Part III, 55–67.

[13] For the most recent and comprehensive account of these theatres, see Giuliana Ricci, "Il teatro del primo Rinascimento," *Teatro d'Italia* (Milano, 1971), 73–105.

cording to the principles of common practice," which indicates that he was cognizant of what was going on around him. This is especially true regarding the technical practices he describes in the *Costruzione*.

We learn the most about Fabrizio Carini Motta, the man, from his own writings. His remarks reveal an intelligent, conservative, prideful perfectionist who longed for the good old days. Statements such as "Those who direct the work of creative individuals for the most part do not understand" or "to lose the glory of one's own creative intentions on account of another's bad work" (in the *Trattato*) disclose an apprehensive and cynical attitude toward those for whom Motta worked. Yet, his constant concern for the welfare of those who worked for him and his continuous emphasis on the "smooth operation" (as revealed in the *Costruzione*) suggest a knowing personality who understood how to achieve the best results from his assistants with a minimum of difficulty. The key to Motta's personality is revealed in his concluding remarks "To the Reader" (in the *Trattato*) in which he reveals an almost fatalistic acceptance of the incompetence of those in charge. "I have this genius," he explains, "and to fight against it would be like swimming upstream, a revocation of talent given to me by nature and genius." Not the words of an immodest man, but one confident, even a little arrogant, of his knowledge and abilities.

Finally, as prefect of theatres to the Gonzaga court during the last quarter of the seventeenth century, Fabrizio Carini Motta was working with the facility and expertise of the traditional Italian theatre artists who were to dominate the European court theatres well into the nineteenth century, those artists who worked simultaneously as theatre architect, scene designer, and stage machinist, such as Motta's contemporaries Gaspare Vigarani, Ludovico Burnacini, Francesco Santurini, and the Mauro brothers. Furthermore, there can be little doubt that had Motta worked in Venice or in a theatre of a more respectable court than the Mantovan court during the twilight years of the brilliant Gonzaga dynasty, Fabrizio Carini Motta would have emerged just as illustrious as his more renowned contemporary, Giacomo Torelli, or even his successors, the Bibiena family.

Trattato sopra la struttura de'Theatri e scene

The *Trattato sopra la struttura de'Theatri e scene che a nostri giorni si custumano e delle Regole per far quelli con proportione secondo l'Insegnamento della pratica Maestra Commune al Fabrico Carini Motta. Architetto del Serenissima di Man-*

tova. Consacrato al Merito Sublime dell'Altezza Serenissima Isabella Clara Arch-duchessa d'Austria, Duchess di Mantova (Treatise on the Structure of Theatres and Scenes, as is customary in our times, with the Rules of Proportion for making them according to the Teachings of the Practices of our Contemporary Masters, by Fabrizio Carini Motta, Architect to His Highness of Mantova. Dedicated with Sublime Respect to Her Highness, Isabella Clara, Arch-duchess of Austria, Duchess of Mantova) was published in 1676.[14] It has been suggested that Carini Motta wrote and dedicated the *Trattato* to Duke Carlo IV's mother, the archduchess of Austria and Mantova, because he looked to her for support against the criticism his work allegedly had generated in the court previous to publication.[15] His rebuttal to his critics is apparent in his address to Her Highness and his remarks to the reader.

A small volume of twenty-four pages and fourteen line drawings, the fifteen chapters in the *Trattato* are devoted to several theatre projects similar to theatres already prevalent early in the seventeenth century. Although earlier writers such as Sebastiano Serlio, Nicola Sabbattini, and Joseph Furttenbach have described theatre auditoriums in sections of commentaries on Vitruvius, technical manuals on stagecraft or books on recreation, Motta's volume is unique as the first volume to treat the theatre auditorium as a separate edifice. The *Trattato* is a prototype in the genre of architectural literature.

The volume contains detailed instructions on how to lay out several types of theatres: theatre projects similar to those that appeared in Europe soon after theatres began to be regarded as single entities, something more permanent than the structure erected temporarily for a festive event in a great hall, a courtyard, or on the green meadow of a villa. Motta's descriptions are in fact among the very first to suggest an evolution of the theatre form from the aristocratic structures of the intellectual academies of the Renaissance courts that attempted to imitate the theatres of classical antiquity, to the class-conscious Venetian playhouses, forerunners of those grandiose opera houses of the eighteenth century. Motta's "theatre of modest intentions" is the first detailed discussion of the layout of the horseshoe-shaped auditorium. He provides the first explanation of the arrangement of the seventeenth-century *palchetti*, predecessor to the eighteenth-century boxes or loges. Some of his auditoria suggest an evolution similar to that from Gian Battista Aleotti's Teatro Intrepidi (Ferrara, 1606), to his Teatro Farnese (Parma, 1618).[16]

---

[14] My commentary on the *Trattato* appeared in *Essays in Theatre*, Vol. 2, No. 3 (May 1984).
[15] See n. 10.
[16] Aleotti's plan for the Teatro degli Intrepidi is in the Archivio di Stato, Modena, Italy; plans for

Introduction

The *Trattato* begins on a most academic note. A theatre, says Motta, is so-called "because it has an auditorium and a stage upon which to perform." The theatres of the Ancients, both Greek and Latin, he observed, were different from those of his time in matters of the "curvature of the rows of seats and the stage jutting out into space upon which the history or fable is performed." As to who should build theatres, this has been clearly explained by Vitruvius and Alberti, from whom, Motta says, "I have taken the principal rules and measurements that have been described with such diligence and logic." Perhaps Motta felt the need for this academic accolade to classical authorities to establish his intellectual credibility with the Mantovan court, but the text that follows is less dependent upon Vitruvius (who is mentioned three times in relation to acoustics, not measurements) and Alberti (who is mentioned only once), than it is upon the later writers Sebastiano Serlio and the Jesuit Father Ignazi Danti, whom Motta quotes from the Vignola edition.[17]

Motta's projects, however, present nothing new or startling, no elaborate concepts based on philosophical theories currently in fashion, such as attributed to the planning of the Teatro Olympico in Sabbionetta.[18] They suggest instead a strong nostalgic feeling for the protocol of the Ducal theatres and the courtly ways of the past (especially with Motta's emphasis on "the Place for the Prince"), with little regard for the growing democratic tenden-

---

the Teatro Farnese (Teatro Salone) are frequently reproduced, notably in *I Teatri di Parma (dal Farnese al Reggio)*, ed. Iov Allodi (Milano, 1969).

[17] Motta must have had numerous editions of Vitruvius at his disposal. And not only Vitruvius but all the current or classical publications on perspective and architecture. Although there were several earlier editions and commentaries, from a historical point of view Motta's best source on classical architecture probably was Daniele Barbaro's commentary in the vernacular with Andrea Palladio's additions: *I diece libri dell'architectura, tradutte a commentari da Mons*, first published in Venice in 1556. Although the first vulgate edition of Alberti's *I dieci libri de l'archittura*, translated by Vincenzo Valgrisis, appeared in Venice in 1546, it is quite likely that Cosimo Bartoli's translation into "lingua Florentina" in Venice in 1565—with its one hundred woodcut illustrations—would have been more useful to Motta. Sebastiano Serlio's *Le Secondo libro de perspective*, with its plans and discussion of a court theatre, first appeared in France in 1545 and Italian editions followed in 1560. The most popular of these by far was Giovanni Domenico Scamozzi's *Tutte le opere di archittetura de Sebastiano Serlio Bolognese*, published in Venice in 1584 and often reprinted thereafter. The Jesuit Giacomo Barozzi da Vignola's *Le Due regole della prospectiva practica del R.P.M. Egnatio Danti* appeared first in Rome in 1583; other editions appeared later but none were as popular as the Vaccatio edition of 1610, which Craig suggests was the edition Motta had access to. See John White, *The Birth and Rebirth of Pictorial Space* (London, 1957). Giuliana Ricci has pointed out the apparent influences of Luigi Sirigatti's *La Pratica di Prospettiva* (Venezia, 1596), *Teatri Italiana*, p. 92.

[18] Kurt W. Foster, "Stagecraft and Statecraft: The Architectural Integration of Public Life and Spectacle in Scamozzi's Theatre in Sabbionetta," *Oppositions*, 9 (1977), 63–87.

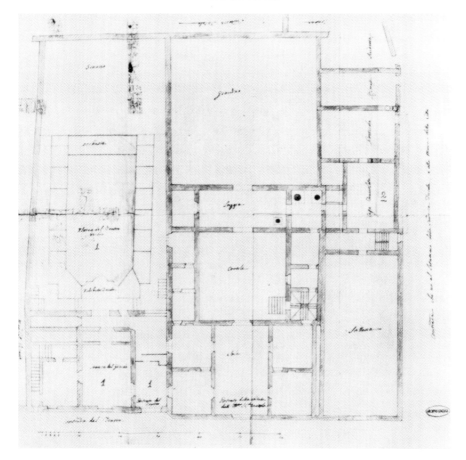

Pianta della zona d'angolo delle attuali piazza Arche e via Teatro Vecchio. Quest'ultima è indicata col nome « Contrada del Teatro ». Col numero 1 sono contrassegnati gli ambienti del Teatro Vecchio, col numero 2 la locanda — dove soggiornò Carlo Goldoni — della ex attrice Giovanna Balletti Calderoni detta « Fragoletta », scritto nella carta « Fraccoletta » (Archivio di Stato di Mantova, busta 3170)

Floor plan of the Teatro dei Comici (later known as the Teatro Vecchio) after Carini Motta remodeled it in 1688. Courtesy of the Archivio di Stato, Mantova, Italy.

cies and the fiscal demands placed on the theatres of his times. Motta's projects, therefore, reflect theatres already in existence. In fact, Stephano della Bella's etching of a theatre erected in Ferrara in 1652 (frontispiece) illustrates precisely the details of the *palchetti* Motta describes in Chapter VIII. Evidence indicates that similar theatres were built in Mantova, which Carini Motta surely saw in his youth.[19]

Among all his details, the most interesting is Motta's placement of "the Place for the Prince" in what Motta labels the "piazza del Theatro" to the rear of his auditorium plan. The "piazza del Theatro" may be regarded as an interesting transitory step between the dais in the middle of the Ducal hall for attending royalty to the king's box in the center of the second tier of the eighteenth-century opera house. Placed at the rear of the auditorium, as in Motta's plan, it is a simple step to raise the piazza del Theatro above the heads of the audience, yet in a position highly visible to most of the spectators.

Not that Motta was unaware of the contemporary design of public playhouses. He built one and remodeled another (as shown in the floor plan of the Teatro Vecchio), but apparently he cared little about the public quality of these theatres. He called them "penny theatre," disdainfully explaining that "one has to pay for every accommodation." From his very first reference to auditoria in the *Trattato,* it is clear that the theatres Carini Motta was most interested in were the private court theatres.

Motta's information about designing single-point perspective settings is quite elementary, with one exception. The information regarding the relationship between the width of the *prospettiva* (backround or backdrop) and the placement of the vanishing point behind the *prospettiva* is new. The distance between the vanishing point and the *prospettiva* should equal the depth of the setting. In addition, the width of the *prospettiva* should never be less than two-thirds the width of the proscenium opening or "the audience will see less than it should." Motta advances a formula to ensure that the greatest

---

[19] A theatre with two tiers of *palchetti,* such as Motta describes in Chapter VIII of the *Trattato,* was erected by Gaspare Vigarani for the royal visit of archdukes Ferdinando Karl and Sigismondo Francesco and the archduchess Anne d'Medici of Austria in May 1652 (*Feste celebrate in Mantova alla ventua de'Serenissimi Archiduchi Ferdinando Carlo, Sigismondo Francesco D'Austria et Archiduchessa Anna Medici . . . Breve narrazione d'Angelo Tarachia,* Mantova, 1652), which Carini Motta must have seen in his youth. Motta himself supplied the scenery and machinery for the *Festa di Mantua* that was held in a similar outdoor theatre. Stephano della Bella's theatre (frontispiece), which, incidentally, was built for the state visit of the same royal trio in Ferrara the previous month, illustrates many of the characteristics and elements Motta describes.

number of the audience will see the greatest part of the settings, information not usually found in other seventeenth-century texts on perspective.

Despite its title, the *Trattato* does not contain specific information on how theatres were constructed in terms of wood and stone or carpentry and masonry. Some construction principles are mentioned, although almost as an afterthought. The *Trattato* is a book about the layout of theatre auditoria with some general comments about the requisites of the stagehouse and abbreviated instructions on how to lay out perspective settings. The emphasis is on the shape and characteristics of theatre auditoria that may be classified, even at the time of publication, as historical types.

Architectural and theatre historians have consistently ignored Fabrizio Carini Motta and the *Trattato*. He is not mentioned in any contemporary theatre history text in English. He is not even mentioned in the Italian *Enciclopedia della Spettacolo*. In 1906 Martin Hammitzsch examined Motta's plans in his survey of the development of the Renaissance and baroque court theatres (*Der Moderne Theaterbau I: Der Hofische Theaterbau*, Berlin, 1906), and forty years later Helene Leclerc repeated Hammitzsch's remarks verbatim (*Les origini italiennes d'architecture theatrale moderne*, Paris, 1946). Robert Aloi mentions Motta in his survey of the horseshoe-shaped auditorium (*Esempi architettura par lo spettacolo*, Milano, 1958), but Giuliana Ricci (*Teatri d'italia*, Milano, 1971) ignores the *Trattato* as do both Donald Mullin (*Development of the Playhouse*, Berkeley, 1970) and George Izenour (*Theatre Design*, New York, 1977).

The obscurity of the *Trattato* is attributed to the supposition that it was originally printed on an inferior grade of paper in a limited edition of about fifty copies, most of which have since disappeared.[20] Copies of the original edition exist in the Avery Architectural Library of Columbia University, the Morgan Library in New York (originally in the theatre collection of the late Donald Oenslager), the Munich Staatbibliothek, and the Rondel collection d'Arsenal in the Bibliotheque Nationale in Paris. Edward A. Craig owns a copy and some still exist in Italy.

In 1973, due mainly to the efforts of Edward A. Craig, the Archivio del Teatro Italiano of the University of Rome reprinted the *Trattato* with the original drawings, but with a modernization of punctuation and spelling in the original text and an introduction, notes, and theatre plans of the period

---

[20] See n. 10.

Introduction

(in Italian) by Craig.[21] Craig, who was unhappy with the emendations in the 1972 edition, privately published a handsome photostat copy of the original 1676 edition with the identical notes, introduction, and plans of the reprint edition (in English) under the misnomer *Baroque Theatre Construction* (Haddenham, Bucks, England: Bledlow Press, 1982). Only Craig's subtitle, "A Study of the Earliest Treatise on the Structure of Theatres by Fabrizio Carini Motta, Architect and Scene Designer at the Court of Mantua, 1676," indicates the true nature of the subject matter. Since the appearance of the reprint edition, Carini Motta's theatre plans from the *Trattato* appear with growing frequency in exhibitions of theatrical art arranged yearly by the Italians for the benefit of summer tourists.

Finally, although theatres far more elaborate than those Motta illustrates in the *Trattato* existed at the time of publication, his work should not be dismissed simply as a discussion of antiquated theatre projects (which is the opinion of some contemporary architectural historians). The *Trattato* is as much a genuine source of information about seventeenth-century theatre architecture as Nicola Sabbattini's *Pratica di fabricar scene e machine ne'teatri* (Ravenna, 1638) is a source on Italian stage machinery, although both describe material in existence for several decades previous to publication. Motta's practicality about how things should be done has a contemporary ring and there is nothing antiquated about Carini Motta's pragmatism.[22]

Construzione de teatri e machine teatrali

The *Costruzione de teatri e machine teatrali di Fabrizio Carini Motta, Ingeg⁴ ed Architetto del Sere^mo Duca di Mantova*, 1688 (Construction of theatres and theatrical machines by Fabrizio Carini Motta, Engineer and Architect to His

---

[21] Fabrizio Carini Motta, *Trattato sopra la struttura de'Teatri e scene,* Introduzione, note e piante di teatri dell'epoca di Edward A. Craig (Milano: Edizione Il Polililo, 1972). Craig's introduction to the 1972 reprint edition unfortunately has been reprinted as the biographical data on Fabrizio Carini Motta in the *Dizionario Biografio Italiana* (Rome: Institute della Enciclopedia Italiana, 1977). Unfortunate, because Craig's information is not always accurate.

[22] Although unrelated to Motta's treatise on theatre architecture it should be noted that Motta also wrote a treatise on the five orders of classical architecture according to the "magnificent codice of [Leon Battista] Alberti." The two parts of this unpublished, undated manuscript are in the Biblioteca Trivulziana (codices 220 and 221) in the Castello Sforza in Milan. The first section describes the symmetry and how to design the separate parts of the Tuscan, Doric, Ionic, Corinthian, and Composite orders, with some critical observation. The second section is a small folio of scala drawings illustrating the size and proportions of the five orders, including separate drawings for the individual parts such as the bases, columns, and cornices. In octavo, 90 pages and 24 line drawings.

Introduction

Serene Highness Duke of Mantova, 1688) exists in an unpublished manuscript dated 1773 in the Campori collection in the Biblioteca Estense in Modena, Italy. It appears that Carini Motta prepared the manuscript about the same time he was renovating the old Teatro dei Comici in Mantova. Not only do the dates coincide but many of Motta's statements, such as "some people say I vary the methods," are in the active voice or present tense, implying immediate action or one just accomplished and suggesting that he is describing current activities.

No evidence exists to indicate why the manuscript was never published, nor why it was copied in 1773 or who the copyist was, although the manuscript has been authenticated as a copy of the original. A connection might be made with the Mantova artist Giovanni Cadioli, who in 1755 recorded in detail the character of the changed Teatro dei Comici after Carini Motta's renovations of 1688.[23] Cadioli's description of the operation of the front curtain of the Teatro Vecchio (as the Teatro dei Comici was known in 1755) is a word-for-word duplication of Motta's description of the operation of a similar curtain in the *Costruzione*. Perhaps Cadioli copied the *Costruzione* as well as recorded the details of the transformed Teatro dei Comici.

The *Costruzione* consists of twenty-three discourses and fourteen plates of twenty-three diagrams illustrating Motta's explanations. Although isolated seventeenth-century drawings and designs exist to picture some of Motta's procedures, the *Costruzione* is the first to put together diagrams and written explanations. It is the first study to treat in a comprehensive way the structure and layout of the Italian stagehouse and its equipment. Motta does not include in his explanations any special effects or exotic machinery; his equipment is such that Motta's contemporaries would expect to find in a well-equipped stagehouse.

In a sense, the *Costruzione* is an extension of the *Trattato,* for Motta refers back to the *Trattato* on several occasions. Thus, a knowledge of what Motta says in the *Trattato* is helpful in understanding much of what Motta says later. However, in the case of his section "On Things Necessary for the Stage" in the *Trattato* (Chapter IV), it is only after one has read Motta's explanation of the same material in the *Costruzione* that the terse *Trattato* text becomes clear. Realistically, if the word stagehouse were substituted for

---

[23] Details of the renovation of the Teatro dei Comici are to be found in Giovanni Cadioli's original manuscript in the *Archivio Gonzaga,* busta 3170 H VII, c 21–24, entitled "Descrizione del Teatro Vecchio in Mantova, 26 Marzo, 1755."

the word theatre in the title, it would reflect a truer indication of the contents of the *Costruzione*.

Motta lays out the requisite for an adequate stagehouse—dimensions and equipment—from the substage area to the stage and from the stage floor to the loft or "grid" area above the stage. He explains the wing-chariot system in detail (with the ladder guides and poles), for changing the wings, including the use of chariots to change the *prospettiva* or background. These include several contemporary variations. He explains the arrangement and operation of various kinds of borders and ceiling pieces and the border-chariot system to move them, including some sophisticated variations. He diagrams the layout of the tracks that carry flight machines above the stage and discusses methods of moving flight machines through hanging borders. He reveals that chariots were used to move set pieces on and off stage and that flats were hung and moved on chariots to form box settings.[24] He offers one of the first explanations of the primitive lighting system used during his lifetime. And finally, as Motta discusses the various arrangements of the mechanical components, he suggests variations of his systems for larger and smaller stagehouses than what he considered ideal.

The *Costruzione* is far more sophisticated than Nicola Sabbattini's *Pratica fabricar scene e machine ne teatri* (Ravenna, 1638), revealing just how far the technology of stage machinery had advanced in the ensuing fifty years. If the *Trattato* describes theatre plans somewhat old-fashioned by the time it was published, the same cannot be said about the information in the *Costruzione,* for it is up to date. Observations by contemporary tourists attest to this fact. The mechanical systems Motta endorses he obviously knew very well, for his explanations disclose a thorough understanding of a variety of technical problems. The *Costruzione* reveals Carini Motta as a most knowing stage machinist.

As a technical director in charge of many stagehands upon whom Motta was dependent for the "smooth operations" he constantly calls for in the *Costruzione,* Motta reflects an astute knowledge of how to handle men. His perception that "pleasant working conditions . . . in ample space" are vital if they (the stagehands) are to accomplish the intricate and coordinated operations necessary to conduct the involved scene shifts or to guide the movements of a complicated cloud machine through its maneuvers are explanatory

[24] Carini Motta's information about box settings appears in my discussion "New Evidence on the Origins of the Box Set," *Theatre Survey,* 21 (November 1980), 2.

Line drawing of cloud machines created by Carini Motta for the *Festa di Mantua*, 1674. Courtesy of the Biblioteca Communale, Mantova, Italy.

of this attitude. (Note the illustration depicting Motta's cloud machines.) Because of the ever-increasing number of stagehands necessary to handle the multi-scene productions that proliferated during the seventeenth century, Motta's concern for convenient working conditions for his crews to ensure smooth operations reflects his managerial skills.

If one is to discount the naivete of most of Sabbattini's explanations (many of which seem to be nothing more than explanations of ingenious miniature models utilized at the rear of the perspective scenes in the intermezzi), the *Costruzione* is the first comprehensive study of stage machinery of significance. Several centuries are to pass before we have similar studies of importance, such as Clement Contant and Joseph de Filippi's *Parallele des Principaux Theatres Moderne de L'Europe et des Machines Theatrales Francaise, Allemande et Anglaise* (Paris, 1860), Fredrich Kranich's *Buhnentechnik der Ge-*

genwart (Berlin and Munich, 1929), and Harold Burris-Meyer and Edward Cole's *Theatres and Auditoriums* (New York, 1949).

When one assimilates the information from the *Trattato* and the *Costruzione,* an accurate picture of the seventeenth-century stagehouse and its equipment evolves for the first time. Furthermore, Fabrizio Carini Motta's detailed explanations reflect his dual role as theatre architect and stage machinist; what today—in the image of a Lee Simonson or a Jo Mielziner—we would call a theatre consultant.[25]

---

[25] As this book goes to press I have received information about two recent studies on Motta by Italian scholars. Maria Francesco Lio, "Fabrizio Carini Motta: Costruzione de'teatri e machine teatrali—Un trattato inedito de scenotecnica seicentesca," thesis directed by Elena Tamburini, Citta Universitaria, Roma, 1984–85; and Guiliana Ricci, "Note sull 'attivita di Fabrizio Carini Motta, architetto teatrale e scenotenico," in *Il Seicento nell'arte e nella cultura con riferimento a Mantova* (Milano, 1985), 148–63.

TRATTATO

SOPRA LA STRVTTVRA DE

THEATRI, E SCENE,

Che à noſtri giorni ſi coſtumano, e delle Regole per far quelli con proportione ſecondo l'Inſegnamento della pratica Maeſtra Commune

DI FABRICIO CARINI MOTTA

Architetto del Sereniſſimo di Mantoua

CONSACRATO

Al Merito Sublime dell' Altezza Sereniſſima

ISABELLA CLARA

ARCIDVCHESSA D'AVSTRIA DVCHESSA

DI MANTOVA

Treatise on the Structures
of Theatres & Scenes

As is customary in our times,
and with the Rules of Proportions according to the Teachings
of the Practices of our Contemporary Masters

by Fabrizio Carini Motta

Architect to His Highness of Mantova
Dedicated
with Sublime Respect to Her Highness
ISABELLA CLARA
Archduchess of Austria
Duchess of Mantova

In Guastalla, by Alessandro Giavazzi, Ducale Printer
With permission of the Court. 1676

[Translation by Orville K. Larson]

Treatise on the structure of theatres and scenes

Serene Highness

I bring to the feet of Your Very Serene Highness this small tribute not only as an example of enthusiastic genius but as the respectful fruit of the duty Your Beneficent Patronage has conferred upon me which obliges me to demonstrate that Your trust in me has not been unfruitful. I know how much this work is lacking in comparison with Your own standards, lacking in excellence because it is a deformed miscarriage of an obscure genius. However, I do not fear that this will be unpleasant to the intelligent eyes of Your Highness. I know that one should place at the feet of the Muses works that are wiser and more enlightening but the glorious name to which this book is dedicated will supply the radiance this work lacks. Nor will it fade into obscurity while the light of this Austrian name shines upon it, whose activities and clairvoyance as the most intelligent queen of the double-eagle of Austria, sustaining more than one crown, constantly engenders great admiration among her subjects under its many suns. Under the royal wings of the eagle, just as the Romans, I hope to continue my felicitous patronage and most assuredly my post. Thus, I do not fear to place the art of building, concentrating on the erection of machines, under the talons of the Royal Bird, who, although the minister of thunder and lightning, makes certain by the generosity of its spirit not to discourage but to cultivate the arts. This I know and thus I hope for the Sovereign protection of Your Serene Highness, at whose feet I kneel and bow, as in my ambitious humility it is my lot to glorify myself. Of V.A.S.

Humble, Devoted and Obedient Servant
Fabrizio Carini Motta

To the Gracious Reader

I wish to appear in the theatre of the world no longer as an engineer of machines but as a player at work. I recite my part not because by the light of my pen do I hope to enhance my name by this change of scene but by my words to remove myself from the dangers my actions expose me to daily. It is unfortunate that those who direct them, lacking in understanding because of others' bad works, stifle the artisan's creative intentions. Moreover, this, in my opinion, is why so few dedicate themselves to so noble a profession. But, for all these difficulties and problems it should not fail to attract geniuses; attempts, in spite of the difficulties, to avail themselves of such a delightful profession. However, the fact is that in the hands of a bad mercenary, commoners, who in the face of Nobility and Princes, turn everything into disaster through negligence and carelessness, turn the most experienced from working in this profession. However, be that as it may, I have this genius, and to fight against it would be like swimming upstream, a revocation of the talent given to me by nature and genius. Therefore, I began to write this treatise not to teach others (which is the work of a master and not an undisciplined mind such as mine), and not only to show how much work and attention goes into these studies (which are the subject of much criticism), but, if you will learn, to understand this ingenious art, and pray for me to the Almighty.

Be Well.

A Comparison of the Theatres of Our Times with Those of the Ancients

Chapter I

(1)* It is not my intention to dwell upon who should build theatres, or in what manner, inasmuch as that has been clearly explained by Vitruvius in Book V, Chapter III, and by Leon Battista Albert in Book VIII, Chapter VII. Although those of the Ancients, either Greek or Latin, are different from those in use today, there are similarities in various parts, and from these I have taken the principal rules and measurements, which have been described with such diligence and such logic.

Among the similarities: first the available space in the middle, the curve of the *gradi*,[1] the *palchetti*,[2] which can serve as the foundation for the *gradi*, and finally to return to the first, the position of the *gradi, palchetti,* and the stage jutting out into space, upon which the history or fable is to be performed.

---

*Numbers in parentheses in the margins indicate page numbers in the first edition of the *Trattato*.

[1] *Gradi* are rows of backless benchlike seats, consisting only of the riser and the seat, without any delineation for individual seats. Generally, these rows continue along the sides and rear of the auditorium and are arranged in tiers; the second higher than the first, the third higher than the second, and so on.

[2] The Italian terms *palco, palchetto,* and *palchetti* (plural) are used today to mean box or boxes in a

Of Things That Are Necessary in the Theatre

Chapter II

Before beginning the description of the theatre, so-called because it has an auditorium and a stage upon which to perform, I shall speak first of some things that are generally very familiar and necessary.

First, many entrances and exits are necessary in a theatre, namely to empty it quickly without causing confusion as to which are entrances and which are exits.

The entrances and stairways, most of which are made of wood, should always be placed as far away from the stage as possible in order not to disturb the performing actors by the noise of those ascending and descending, as there are always people moving around, some by necessity and others "just for fun."

It is a very good practice, whenever possible, to place the doors, steps, and corridors leading up to the *gradi* or *palchetti* away from the performers, that is to say, beyond the walls of the *gradi* or *palchetti* but not so they interfere with the general passageways. Away from the auditorium, however, so that the noise of the people walking in the corridors will not interfere with hearing the performers.

The *gradi* or *palchetti* must be arranged in such a manner that everyone will be able to see and hear comfortably. (2)

A theatre must provide places for the wardrobe, for supplies, as well as dressing rooms for the actors to which they can come and go without being seen by the audience, especially when they are dressing for a performance. The stagehouse should be as spacious as possible because even other areas are needed in order to change scenery during the performances and to provide backstage space for the stage machinery such as the wings, cars, substage machines, as well as others that are sometimes necessary, in order that

---

theatre auditorium, a usage that became common in the eighteenth century. However, the term *palchetti*, as Carini Motta uses it in 1676, means something quite different. As Motta uses the term it refers to the tiers on the auditorium sides as Stephano della Bella's etching of a theatre erected in Ferrara in 1652 (frontispiece) illustrates. Sometimes several rows of *gradi* were set below and in front of the first level of *palchetti*, and occasionally (as in the frontispiece) rows of *gradi* were placed above the highest level of *palchetti*. The posts that support the various levels of *palchetti* on the open side tend to indicate that the *palchetti* were divided into sections when in reality they were not. Passageways behind the *gradi* on each level allowed the spectators to move along easily to and from their seats.

they might disappear suddenly or rise without interrupting any other operations or persons.

The *gradi* or *palchetti* should be divided into three sections, in such a manner that the nobility are located apart from the lower classes, namely, in the most noble places, which are the lowest or on the auditorium floor, where, for their convenience, they can enter and exit separately. The lesser nobility are placed in the middle sections and the commoners at the very top.

General Rules for Seeing in the Theatre
Chapter III

A general rule to be observed in all theatres is always to arrange the seats in a semicircular fashion to the stage, when circumstances do not dictate an angular form, even for those with *gradi* or *palchetti*, for reasons Vitruvius cites in Book V, Chapter III: that the noises move through the air in a circular fashion rather than spherically. I shall call the semicircular area of the auditorium floor the *piazza del theatro* (as did Serlio), upon which the seats for the Prince and principals of the court are arranged.

The first row of *gradi* does not rise from the auditorium floor (which I shall call the *scena*) but begins on a raised portion or a parapet between 57 and 76 inches[3] above the auditorium floor. The stage shall be raised to a height corresponding to that of the parapet.

The risers of the *gradi* that begin upon the parapet should be 19 inches high and the seats at least as wide. When there is ample room, make the seats 25 inches wide.

At various intervals in the *gradi* the seat of a row should be made double the width of the others so it can serve as an aisle to make walking easier. There should be three aisles: one before that first row, that is to say, on the (3)   floor of the parapet, one in the middle and, one behind the top row.

---

[3] A Mantovan *brazza* or *braccio* —Motta uses both terms—is 46 centimeters or slightly more than 19 inches. An *oncia* is 1½ inches. Motta gives dimensions using both terms. In addition, when speaking about the proportions of various parts of the theatre and their relationships, Motta often describes them in terms of "units," which he explains consists of three *brazza*, or 57 inches. To arbitrarily transpose these units into feet and inches often destroys the continuity and sense of Motta's statements. Therefore, for reasons of clarity, only Motta's dimensions given in *brazza* or *oncie* are translated into feet and inches. When assimilated, these give all the pertinent dimensions as the Tables of Measurements from the *Trattato* and the *Costruzione* indicate. Readers are cautioned, however, that there are inconsistencies between some measurements in the *Trattato* and the *Costruzione* that the translator has not always tried to adjust. To do so would only add to the confusion.

Treatise on the structure of theatres and scenes

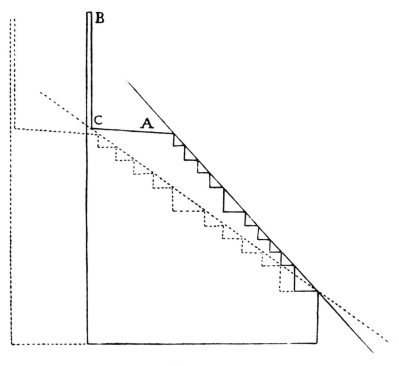

Figure A

When the riser of the row behind the rows that serve also as aisles (which I shall call the *piazzeta*) is the same dimension as the width of the aisle row, then the front edge of all the *gradi* are tangent to a line drawn from the front edge of the parapet to the front edge of the uppermost row of seats as indicated in Figure A. Then the voice will rise evenly and nothing will impede it, as would happen if it were constructed differently. This Vitruvius teaches in the aforementioned book and chapter. Then, behind the highest row of seats, that is, on the level indicated as A, a *loggia* or at least a parapet should be arranged, extending to the semicircular wall that encloses the rear of the auditorium, as the line BC indicates.

The present drawing illustrates how the risers of the *gradi* must be arranged in order for all of them to conform to the straight line in the diagram. As the line bridges the *gradi*, the other proportions become apparent.

The distance between the stage opening and the beginning of the side *gradi* or *palchetti* should be between 6 feet 4 inches and 8 feet 6 inches wide,

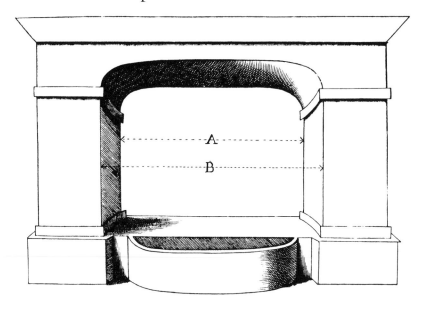

Figure B

depending on the size of the stage and the auditorium, as the designs indicate.

It is customary for many to join the *gradi* or *palchetti* to the wall of the proscenium opening, but when this is the case they are so close that they dominate completely the scene at the sides of the proscenium, which is not good. In order to escape this imperfection, it is wise to make a deep proscenium opening, not so thick that it can't be used, no wider than the front wing, because when it is, those flanking the proscenium opening are unable to see completely. It even causes problems for the master painters who must decorate the proscenium, for most of the space is lost when the sides join the opening. It is not amiss to show how similar theatres are arranged and proportioned.

The front ends of the *gradi* or *palchetti,* parallel to the proscenium opening, should not be wider than 5 feet 8 inches and no less than 4 feet 9 inches. Then the side *gradi* will angle back to the points of intersection at the edges of the semicircular *loggia,* which is 30 feet 8 inches wide, thus providing a diagonal line of sight so that the spectators in the *gradi* or *palchetti* will have an unobstructed view of the stage, specially those in the rear.

The *proscenio* opening is made in the face of the wall that forms the front of the stage and orchestra. The *occhio della scena* on the opposite side is formed by the extremity of the thickness of the *proscenio* opening, as shown in Figure B. In this drawing, A indicates the *occhio della scena* and B the opening of the *proscenio*.

When constructing a theatre with *palchetti,* the placement of the first level is exactly the same. They are set upon the parapet one level above the other, and they are normally 6 feet 4 inches high, namely, of sufficient height that a man can stand comfortably when the *palchetti* do not contain *gradi.* When *gradi* are included (as I shall show in the designs) then the *palchetti* must be 8 feet high in order for people to see and to accommodate a large number comfortably.

The width of the theatre determines the major measurements of the structure. The width is divided into 12 equal parts.

The opening on the parapet that is the front of the stage should be seven-twelfths of the width. The height of the opening should not be more than four-fifths of the width (that is to say, divide the opening into 5 parts and make the height 4 parts of this), and no less than three-quarters of the width.

A very good proportion is to divide the opening into 9 parts and make the height seven-ninths of the width, which is the proportion I use in my designs.

To achieve the best proportions, the distance from the front of the stage to the parapet of the *piazza del theatro* should be at least fourteen-twelfths of the width of the theatre and no less than twelve and two-thirds.

The *piazza del theatro* should be large, at least half the width of the theatre.   (4)

The size of the *loggia,* or rear section of the auditorium, is relative to the arrangement of the *gradi* or *palchetti,* but when there are *gradi* the best proportion is eight-twelfths of the width of the theatre.

The opening of the *proscenio* must be larger, that is to say, wider than that of the *occhio della scena,* by one-twelfth part of the width of the theatre, and the height, one-half part; that is to say, it is one part wider. The top corners of the opening are rounded off in a circular form, which because of the thickness thus creates a niche, necessary for reasons of singing, as mentioned at the beginning of this chapter.

The aforementioned thickness should not be less than 4 feet 9 inches and no wider than 9 feet 6 inches, that is, from the *occhio della scena* to the beginning of the orchestra in which the players and speakers who walk onstage (that is to say, those who do not have to depend on machines) perform. Voices that are usually restricted by this thickness gain added projection toward the audience because of the cavity of the opening. Others who perform here to the accompaniment of the orchestra are heard just as beautifully as in the orchestra when they are seen and heard in that space. This is a most important and necessary point.

Some say that performing in the aforementioned space is to come out of the stage picture and consequently not be a part of the scene, but in order to be heard in the auditorium, it is best to do this, a lesser evil than to be behind the *scena* and not be heard.

The orchestra should not be more than 6 feet 4 inches deep nor narrower than 4 feet 9 inches.

Even if the summit of the circular opening is practically drawn by hand, I have illustrated how to make it symmetrically and how to foreshorten the opening pleasantly.

The height of the theatre, that is, from the auditorium floor to the ceiling, should not be greater than the length of the theatre, nor should it be less than two-thirds of the length. The very best proportion will be to make the height of the auditorium four-fifths of the length of the theatre.

Make the side walls of the theatre curve gracefully into the ceiling in a circular fashion so that the ceiling covers the auditorium like the half of an egg (as I have described the summit of the *occhio della scena* and the *proscenio*).

There must be a space above the soffit, that is, between it and the rafters of the roof, at least high enough for a man to walk about freely, which occurs often. Even space for the various machines, such as the drums and capstans, in such a way as to keep the area above the stage free as possible in order to move about quickly to operate the machines, ceilings, and whatever else occurs.

It is necessary to build a stage loft with beams fitted together and bolted to the walls to support and strengthen the stage loft so that the catwalks are safe, and the structure strong enough to stand the force to stop safely the implements mentioned above.

On Some Things Necessary for the Stage
Chapter IIII

(6) Once the site of the stage has been established and its length, the slope of the stage floor must be determined; no more than a twentieth part and no less than a sixteenth, which finally will be a level rising one-twentieth part at the most, one-sixteenth at the least, that is to say, divide the length of the stage

into 16 or 20 parts and raise it to one of these. Serlio does not give a ratio for his slope, but our way is very quick and expeditious.

One must excavate below the stage, that is to say, create a substage area below the streets, in order to be able when necessary to create the sea and machines without interfering with the scene changes.

The height of the stage above the stage floor must be as great as that above the ceiling in order to have room for the machinery. I do not prescribe a height for the stagehouse because the higher it is the better it will be for the diversity of operations that will have to take place therein. It is very true that distance between the top of the *occhio della scena* and the rafters of the roof should never be less than the height of the opening of the *occhio della scena*.

It will be advantageous to line the inside of the roof with boards, lining it like the inside of a large earthen jug. First, in order to hold the voices inside but also to keep out the wind and frigid winter air as well as the fiery rays of the sun, all of which succeed in contributing immensely to the damage of the operations as well as to the performers.

Below stage (that is, below the stage level where the scene changes are made), a subterranean area deep enough for a man to walk around comfortably must be arranged, of a length at least to the end of the second perspective. This substage area will be excellent, even necessary, for the various kinds of substage machinery, such as for seascapes, marine monsters, infernos, as well as other necessary operations. It also contains the support pylons, made of stone, that carry the master joists or beams of the stage floor. These pylons must be so placed as not to obstruct the passageways of the substage streets or of any of the operations, especially not of the chariots.

The stage floor must be trapped so that the traps can be opened, not only when it is necessary for the mechanical effects to be raised or lowered, but also when it is necessary to air out the substage area to prevent the wooden beams from rotting.

For the best insurance that the substage joists or beams will not rot, they must be coated with pitch or tar, even the ends of the timbers used for the (7) *gradi* or *palchetti* that are sunk into the ground or set into the walls should be coated with pitch, as well as those for the stagehouse and the scaffolds for the machines, to make sure they will last a very long time.

Above the stage are the *gargami*[4] for the machines, suspended so high in

---

[4]The seventeenth-century Italian word *gargamo* (*gargami*, plural) was used to mean any kind of a guide, track, or channel in which objects were pulled, pushed, or moved by whatever means from one point to another. Motta uses the term here to describe a track of two parallel rafters or beams,

the air by rods or slender poles that they are masked by the sky. These *gar-gami* are arranged over each street, aligned parallel to the streets so the machinery can carry whatever is necessary in such a way that they can be used unencumbered. These same *gargami* are so constructed that when they are not needed in the operations, they can be adapted to serve as crossover catwalks from one side of the stage loft to the other, covered with hinged sections of flooring that can be opened and closed, sections that do not interfere with either the movements of the carts for the flight machines or with the lowering of the machines themselves to the stage floor below.

These *gargami* are so arranged that they can part in the middle when it is necessary for a machine overhead to move through them as it moves forward toward the audience carrying whatever is necessary.

Above the stage area there are several sets of corridors or catwalks. The lowest of these is on the same level as the aforementioned *gargami*. These catwalks are separated, one above the other, so that one can move aloft freely. The ladders to reach the various levels should be so positioned that they will not be an obstruction but will facilitate the work with ease.

When the spaciousness of the stagehouse will permit, there may even be other sets of *gargami* above the first, with corridors or catwalks, as I have described, to accommodate more machines.

The ceilings must be able to move in the free streets between the *gargami*. They must be able to descend into position and to rise freely in such a manner that they will not impede the machinery or their operations.

Experience has taught me to place the *gargami*[5] for the ceilings slightly out of plumb with the side wings, in such a manner that the ceilings hang behind the side wings slightly, to avoid the difficulties of the ceilings fouling into the wings during the scene changes. When you take the chance of moving the ceilings faster than the side wings difficulties often arise, as the ceiling comes in above the wings yet remaining slightly above and not meeting,

---

with a space between, that served as rails of a track. The machines or carts that contained the winches and other paraphernalia for flying clouds, thrones, chariots, animals, as well as human beings, move along these beams from one side of the stage to the other depending on the action of the flight phenomenon. The ropes or cables suspending the flying objects from the cart on the track moved between the beams of the track.

[5] At this point in his explanation, the *gargami* that Motta is talking about are quite different from the *gargami* he just concluded explaining that support the machines that move across the stage from side to side between the wings. The *gargami* that Motta refers to here are U-shaped channels, set perpendicular to the floor on each side of the stage above the wings. These channels form guides in which the ends of each border slides as it moves up and down.

in some cases creating a most unpleasant sight. Arranging them right above the side wings is surely dangerous, and when it happens it will produce great confusion. But when they are arranged as I have mentioned above, you are assured against such disorders and will not create any bad effects. To the eye, the one will appear united with the other, that is, the side wings with the ceilings.

The sky[6] is so hung that between it and the tops of the wings there is some (8) space for foliage and trees to appear above said wings, not appearing to reach the clouds, except when the frames of the sky borders are hung so low that they conceal the machines and that which is intended for the sides.

These skies must be split so that the copper, iron, or brass wires from which the moving machines are suspended can pass through as they move forward and approach the audience.

On the sides, from the first perspective to the last horizon, passageways or corridors should be constructed on several levels, which will be very convenient in the operations; in order to arrange the winches, drums, and other equipment needed for the machines, cautioning, however, that they be placed in such a way as not to be a hindrance to anyone.

The first wing in the front of the scene is made six-sevenths of the height of the *occhio della scena,* that is to say, divide the height of the opening into seven parts, six of which will be the height of the first wing.

Personages that seem to move, such as men or animals, should not be represented or painted into the setting, but marble or metal is always depicted, as are other similar materials.

We are not able to give a definite width for the streets, that is, the distances between the sets of chariots that make the scene changes onstage, because in the larger theatres they will be wider than in the smaller theatres. However, whatever width is used, in the larger ones as well as the smaller, it will always be best, not only for convenience, to arrange the movements of the chariots on and offstage so as to allow the greatest space in the Heavens for the aerial machines that must pass between them; even for the cars and other items that must come onstage. However, it is not expedient to have the streets less than 3 feet 6 inches wide in the smallest theatres, 4 feet 3 inches wide in the medium, and 5 feet 1 inch wide in the largest theatres.

---

[6] By "sky" Motta is here referring to another kind of border, the sky border that is painted to represent some natural phenomenon of the celestial heavens such as a cloudy, clear, or foreboding sky.

A Method to Design a Theatre According to the Aforementioned Rules

Chapter V

Having heretofore explained the ways, rules, and proportions that must be observed to construct a theatre according to my modest intentions, as I have understood what seems necessary in the practice of a similar profession, it is now my main purpose to designate these, as those for the *gradi* or those for the *palchetti,* with all the proportions indicated.

(9)   First, it is necessary to determine the length and width of the site, which in the case of my plan is 185 feet 3 inches long and 60 feet 10 inches wide, as I have indicated in my design ABCD in Figure I.

If you divide the width of the site, namely the 60 feet, into 12 equal parts, as I have indicated by line E-F, each part will be 5 feet. Thirteen of these to be delegated for the depth of the stage, namely, from the *occhio della scena* to the rear wall of the stagehouse, 59 feet 10 inches long, as indicated by site AECF.[7]

This division of the width of the theatre into 12 parts will give, as stated, almost all the measurements. I caution, however, that when in the divisions I do not specify any other than the usual or simple parts, I always mean them to be a part of the 12, which is the division of the width of the theatre.

The parapet that divides the *piazza del theatro* from the *piazza della scena* is 14 parts wide similar to the width of the stagehouse, as the line G-H indicates. The distance between it and the stage is 70 feet. Then mark the points I and K on the line G-H, with a distance of 2¼ parts between points I-G and K-H. Thus, the length of I-K will be 7½ parts of the usual measurement. Then from the front edge of the parapet, at points I and K, draw the diago-

---

[7] In the *Costruzione* Motta gives this dimension as 15 units. However, it is obvious that when stating the depth of the stagehouse as 13 units deep he is excluding the depth of the proscenium opening (2 units) from his dimension. It is interesting to note that nowhere in either the *Trattato* or the *Costruzione* does Motta speak specifically about the "identity" of the proscenium opening. Is it to be considered a part of the stagehouse and its depth included in the overall dimension of the depth of the stagehouse? Or does this thickness in reality divide the length of the auditorium from the depth of the stagehouse? Motta makes no mention of this in the *Costruzione* in which he constantly speaks of the stagehouse as 15 units deep, without ever mentioning the depth of the proscenium opening. It is only in plan ✣ in Figure X of the *Trattato* that Motta illustrates a proscenium opening in relation to both the stagehouse and the auditorium. As this diagram indicates, he obviously thought of the proscenium opening as a part of the auditorium rather than the stagehouse, which in no way explains the discrepancy between the 13 and 15 units.

FIG: I.

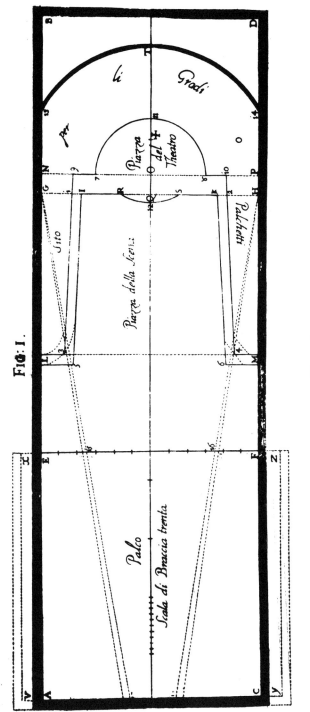

Figure I

31

nal lines, as I have indicated, which will form the *piazza della scena* and the side *gradi* or *palchetti*. To find the ends of the latter, draw the line L-M some distance from E-F, but not more than 5⅓ parts (approximately 27 feet). Then locate points 1 and 2 on the line G-H, with the distance between G-1 and H-2 ½ part or 2 feet 9 inches. The distance between L-3 and M-4 is 1⅕ parts (approximately 5 feet 4½ inches). Draw the lines to connect points 3-1 and 4-2, and from points I and K draw lines I-5 and K-6 parallel to the lines 3-1 and 4-2. Then connect 1-3 and M-4 to form the sides and ends of the *gradi* or *palchetti*, as well as the *piazza della scena*.

And if the sharp angles at 5 and 6 cause problems in the *piazza della scena*, they can be cut off with either a diagonal line as indicated by the dotted line at M or with a curved line as indicated at L, which is in fact the best way as it obstructs the view the least.

To create the *piazza del theatro* draw the line N-P parallel to and one part of the usual measurement beyond the line G-H. Then, from the center point o draw the half circle 7-11-8, with the diameter (7-8) one-half the width of the theatre, or 27 feet 6 inches. Extend the lines 3-1 and 4-2 so they will intersect the line K-P at the points 9 and 10. The line between points 9 and 10 terminates[8] the *piazza del theatro*.

If you wish to make the parapet appear more graceful, the straight edge L-K can be curved as line R-12-S indicates, from the center point ✛. The

(10)

radius ✛-Q is equal to the distance between R-S, which is 3 parts of the usual measurement, or 15 feet.

The back wall of the *loggia* 13-T-14, which will close off the rear of the auditorium, will be 8 parts behind the parapet, namely from Q to T, which is equal to the width of the *piazza del theatro* (7-8), plus one-third. With the radius O-T swing an arc for the *gradi* or *palchetti*. Thus is shown all my thoughts on the design.

The position of the receding wings of the setting onstage is determined first by the width of the *occhio della scena*, which is at least 7 parts, as I have mentioned, or 32 feet 8 inches, as indicated between points 15 and 16 on line E-F. The widest span of vision is the width of the auditorium between G-H. To find the receding angle, draw lines from points G and H, passing through points 15 and 16 on line E-F, extending them onstage until they intersect the

---

[8]Motta's verb "terminates" is confusing. Obviously, Motta means that the line 9-10 would indicate the leading edge of the *piazza del theatro* parapet if the side *gradi* or *palchetti* are extended along the lines 3-9 and 4-10.

prospettiva.[9] The *prospettiva* of the scene can be determined at any parallel points along the diagonal lines 15 and 16 to the rear wall of the stagehouse.[10]

It is always necessary to extend the sides of the stagehouse beyond those of the auditorium, for changing the scenes as much as for the performance, as I have indicated with dotted lines VXYZ, or extended at least as much as one-half the opening on each side from points 15 and 16 (ends of the *occhio della scena*) to the points Y and Z (which are one-half the opening 15-16).

How to Determine the Vanishing Point in Order to Design the Perspective Scenes
Chapter VI

Before putting forth an evaluation, it is necessary to explain and demonstrate how to find and determine the horizon point (vanishing point), which will always work and is very essential in designing settings, in order that in every design everyone in the theatre will be able to see the perspective setting.

The vanishing point, Father Ignazio Danti says in his commentary on the *prospettiva,* in discourse 6, is the end of the visitor's view in which all parallel lines of the linear plan that creates a receding angle will terminate. To find said point in the theatre, Sebastiano Serlio instructs us to draw the line arbitrarily beyond the scene, as far as one-half the length of the depth of the scene and place the vanishing point there. Then, from that point, draw lines to the sides of the *occhio della scena* and the points where these lines will intersect the *prospettiva* will indicate both the contracting angle of the lines of the wings and the ultimate width of the rear perspective, as can be seen in Figure II, namely, the length of the stage V-X, carrying it beyond the end (A-C), as

---

[9] Motta uses several words to indicate the rear shutter, back frame, backdrop, or rear perspective of the setting, which in reality are all the same thing—the rear piece of scenery that closes off the rear part of the setting of either an interior or exterior scene. In the interests of clarity, the Italian word *prospettiva* will be used throughout the translation to indicate this piece of scenery.

[10] The exact translation of the last two lines of this paragraph reads "the lines G-17 and H-18 passing through points 15 and 16 will have diminished on the stage to the narrowest width of the *occhio della scena*. The designation of this scene for the largest width must be drawn from points G and H, passing through points 20 and 12, to points 15 and 16." Inasmuch as Motta failed to indicate points 17, 18, 20, and 21 on his diagram, the literal translation becomes exceedingly garbled. He obviously is thinking of Figure V at this point in his explanation, as all these points are indicated in that drawing.

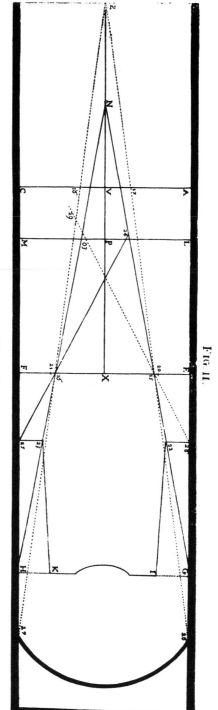

FIG. II.

Figure II

34

indicated by V-Z. Point Z will be the vanishing point from which the lines $\quad$ (11) Z-15 and Z-16 are drawn to the sides of the *occhio della scena*. These lines intersect the *prospettiva* A-C at points 17 and 18. The distance between points 16 and 17 indicates the ultimate width of the *prospettiva* and the narrowest width of the openings between the side wings.

The length of the stage should not exceed two-thirds of the distance between the proscenium opening and the parapet of the *piazza del theatro,* namely, the depth of the stage A-E is no greater than two-thirds of E-G. LEFM indicates the stage and N is the vanishing point. Praise the present rule that has even served me, because by drawing the lines N-G and N-H that intersect the width of the stage opening at points 15 and 16, they traverse the side *gradi* or *palchetti* in such a manner that more than half of the audience sitting on either side can see the vanishing point or the *prospettiva* very well, as is indicated by the lines 22-6 and N-15, and 23-H and H-16. Even the spectators in the very rear of the seats, as indicated by points 25 and 28, will be able to see the opposite sides of the *prospettiva,* as indicated by sight lines 24-25 (passing through point 16).

But when the stage is more than two-thirds the length mentioned above, as the space AEFC indicates, the vanishing point will be Z, from which the lines Z-26 and Z-27 are drawn intersecting the stage opening at points 15 and 16. In this case the sides will lose much of the view as the said lines and points indicate. The same is true from points 28-29. And even when the proscenium opening is wider, most of the audience on the sides will see considerably less of the setting, because what they will see is simply not a view of all that is there.

What has been said regarding a stage opening with a width[11] of the size indicated by the space between points 15 and 16 holds true for an even larger one, as 20-21 indicates.

One notices, too, that when the vanishing point is carried beyond the *prospettiva* a distance equal to the depth of the scene (whatever the distance), the width of the scene on the *prospettiva* will always be one-half the width of the proscenium opening. The stage being LECF and the vanishing point N, drawing the oblique lines, as mentioned and explained, the *prospettiva* (designated as 24-30) will be one-half the width of the opening 15-16. Likewise, when the stage is AECF and the vanishing point is Z, the oblique lines from

---

[11] Obviously, Motta is talking about stage depths at this point, not widths of the proscenium opening. The diagram indicates as much.

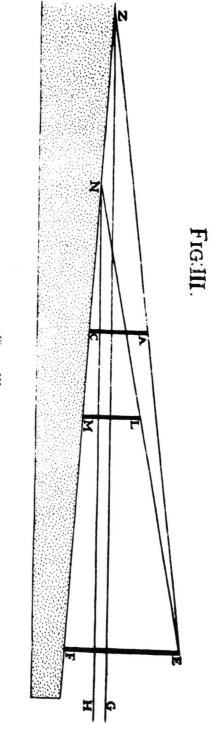

FIG. III.

Figure III

36

Z intersect the ends of the perspective A-C at points 17 and 18. The *prospettiva,* designated as 17-18, will be one-half the opening 15-16.

In the same way when arranging the wings, when the vanishing point is equidistant to the distance from the rear wing to the front of the stage, the last wing will always be one-half the height of the first, namely, as is indicated (12) in Figure III, wherein the vanishing point N is as far from the rear wing L-M as L-M is from the front wing E-F. Draw the line E-N from the point E (top of the first wing) to the vanishing point N. This will determine the height of the rear wing L-M, which will be one-half the height of the front wing E-F. The same holds true between lines E-A and A-Z.

Then, in the same figure, draw a horizontal line from either vanishing points N or Z, as lines N-H and Z-G indicate, and these lines (perpendicular to the horizon line on the *prospettiva*) will serve as the vanishing point in arranging the perspective on any of the wings, or upon whatever else.

The rules described here are extremely workable because all the lines (such as those for the contraction of the scene and for the determination of the height of the wings) all terminate at one point; done naturally considering how things appear to the eye, and from that we learn (as Father Ignazio Danti tells us in Book 5) that things are not only practices just for the reasons discussed above relating to the depth of the stage. There is much more: how the wings diminish, how to build and point the wings, and how to blend them with the vanishing point.

Theatres of today are different from what Serlio illustrated with a large auditorium floor, in regard to the ballets that used them in the same way the Ancients performed other similar festivals in the amphitheatres. (Vitruvius says in Book V, Chapter III, that it was customary to use large stages for the representation of large city squares with great vistas. It was necessary, however, to caution that those who design stages do so in such a way that audiences on the sides can enjoy the best view possible.) However, for the permanent stage in my design AECF, in Figure IIII, extend the parapet I-K to the rear wall of the theatre, and from the points G and H draw lines to infinity, N (vanishing point), that intersect points 15 and 16. When the lines intersect the rear of the stage at points 17 and 18, the oblique lines 15-17 and 16-18 will indicate the position of the various pairs of side wings along those lines.

If the stage is deeper than the permanent stage A-E, say extended to A-G or even a-d, which would provide another quarter of advantage of the length of A-E, it will be necessary to make the proscenium opening larger than al-

37

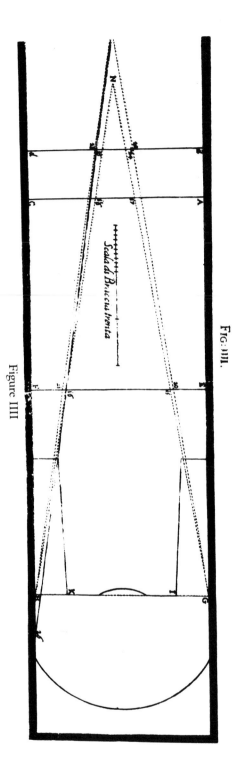

FIG. IIII.

Scala di Bracciu trenta

Figure IIII

38

ready stated, as indicated by points 20 and 21. From points G and H draw lines through points 20 and 21 that intersect the rear wall A-C at points 22 and 23, which will determine the width of the *prospettiva* of the scene.

One must caution, however, that the width of the *prospettiva* must not be less than 3 parts of the *occhio della scena,* that is, the distance between points 22 and 23, but no less than 3 parts of the opening designated by points 21 and 20. The same is true for points 17 and 18 from points 15 and 16.

Every time then that a part of the *prospettiva* diminishes, a part of the *occhio della scena* is also diminished, as can be seen by line 16-26. From Z it (13) passes through point 25 ending at the third part of the width 15-16.

How to Design the Stage from the Narrower Opening of the *Occhio della Scena* to the Front Ends of the *Gradi* or *Palchetti*

Chapter VII

Figure V illustrates a shorter distance between the *proscenio* and the side *gradi* or *palchetti* as well as the shortest distance between said sides and the *occhio della scena* (4 parts of the usual measurement), as indicated by lines E-F and L-M. The front ends of these sides, which are of equal width, are indicated by L-3 and M-4. In order to determine the width of the opening of the *occhio della scena* when the stage is 69 feet 6 inches deep, I have drawn the lines G-N and H-N, passing through points 15 and 16 (indicating the narrower width of the *occhio della scena*) and continuing on to points 17 and 18. The width between these past points is narrower than the distance between points 22-24, which is a third of the *occhio,* which as I have cautioned in the last chapter is not good. In this case, if you use the narrower opening you will lose visibility of some of the stage as the line 13-16-24-V indicates. If you use the larger opening, you will increase the width of the *prospettiva* and you will not decrease the sight lines, as indicated by line G-20-Z.

And when the stage is 80 feet 6 inches deep, it will be necessary to use the larger opening, although you will lose a little of the sight lines, as indicated by lines 13-21-X, intersecting at point 26, which will determine the width of the *prospettiva* for the larger openings.

And if you use the smaller opening, you will lose a greater amount of sight

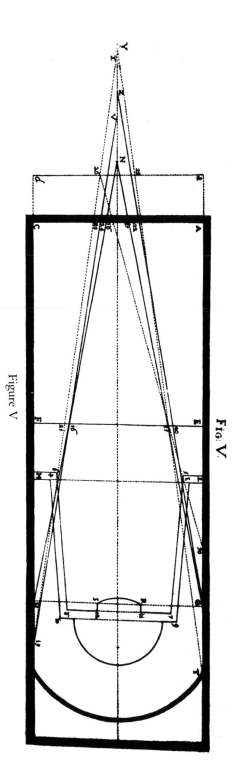

Figure V

Fig: V.

40

lines from the sides, as the line T-15-Y passing through point 25 (edge of *prospettiva*) will indicate.

Because all stage settings are not as deep as I have indicated for the deep stage, I will explain a proportionate depth using a stage of 65 feet deep and indicate the angle of recession or diagonal sight lines, from points G and H to the stage, using, as I have explained, the narrower opening of the *occhio della scena,* which is very necessary. When one creates a setting of a great vista, the wings and borders will align themselves along the line Y-25-15-T, (14) and those sitting on the sides behind the line 30-15-26 will not see as much as those forward of this line.

For the best arrangement of the parapet (of the *piazza del theatro*), it should extend out onto the auditorium floor as shown by points 7-11-R-S-12-8, moving it forward between lines G-H and 9-10, and extending the platform 11-r-s-12 forward toward the vanishing point. This will serve as an extended platform toward the stage.

How to Design the Wings
Chapter VIII

As I have indicated, when designing the wings onstage, they diminish to the vanishing point very sharply, so that the last wing and the *prospettiva* become very small, so small in fact that when an actor appears in front of them, the actor appears much larger than the setting, especially when they emerge through a doorway or an arch. For that reason, care must be taken to make the scene as magnificent as possible in order to produce the best effect, as cautioned, for the very important aforementioned reasons. On that account they should be designed as follows.

Lay out on the floor or on a wall the exact measurement of the stage opening, as shown by rectangle 1-2-3-4 in Figure VI. Then draw the line 5-6 parallel to line 3-4, some distance above line 3-4, that is to say, as a distance previously explained, which is the distance C-O in Figure III.[12] Then in the middle of the line 5-6 mark off the length I-K, equal to the width of the rear perspective (which will be the distance between points 17 and 18 in Figure IIII), and from said points I and K draw lines A and B at right angles to line 5-6 up to infinity. Then mark off the first set of wings E-F as a predetermined

---

[12] C-O is a mistake, since no letter O is indicated in Figure III. It seems likely that C-F is the distance Motta is referring to at this point.

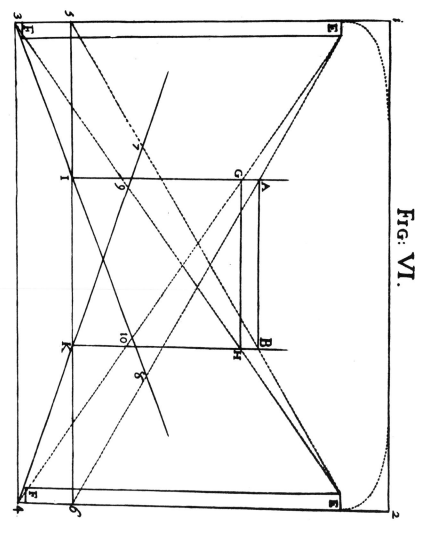

Fig: VI.

Figure VI

42

height, indicating exactly how far onstage they set from the sides of the stage opening (1-3 and 2-4) and how far back from the front of the stage (3-4). Then from points E, the top corner of said first wings, to points 5 and 6 draw the diagonal lines E-5 and E-6. Where these lines intersect the perpendicular lines A-I and B-K, the line A-B will indicate the top edge of the *prospettiva* or horizon, which is indicated in the diagram as A-B-K-I. Finally, from the points F (the opposite corners of the first wings) through the points I and K, draw lines to infinity. The lines E-A, E-B, F-L, and J-K will determine the   (15) height of all other wings and indicate the best angle for diminishing the wings.

At the same time, the points designated for the middle wings 7 and 8 are created by the intersection of lines E-6 and F-8 and the lines E-5 and F-7, that is to say that point 7 indicates the middle wing on side A and point 8 on side B.

When it is desirable to diminish the wings at a sharper angle, all one has to do is draw the lines from points E to 3 and 4 instead of 5 and 6, and where they intersect lines A-I and B-K, at points G and H, the line G-H will indicate the height of the smaller *prospettiva,* and the points 9 and 10, caused by the intersection of lines E-3 and E-4 with lines F-7 and F-8, will indicate the position of the middle wings along lines F-I and F-K. Thus, the edges that are painted on the wings will not appear so sharp and produce a pleasing effect to the eye.

How to Determine the Best Angle
of the *Occhio della Scena*
and Curve of the *Proscenio* [13]

Chapter IX

First, the height of the opening is determined, that is, the principal height of the rotunda or curvature of the opening. This can be determined by dividing the height of the opening into 7 equal parts, using one part, namely, the upper part, in which to shape the opening, as Figure C illustrates representing the *occhio della scena,* in the proportions that I have devised to serve me.

---

[13] This chapter heading is misleading as Motta speaks only of how to determine the curvature of the top of the proscenium opening. He says nothing about the angle of inclination between the *proscenio* and the *occhio della scena.*

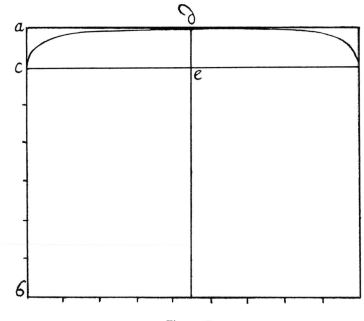

Figure C

For this reason, the height a-b is divided into 7 parts, and a-c is the part within which the curve is circumscribed in the following manner.

Suppose the oblong ABCD in Figure VII is the same proportion as is acde in Figure C, namely, half the length of the width of the opening and one-seventh of the eighth of the same. Said oblong is divided into equal parts, arbitrarily. For example, I have divided it into 10 parts, as seen with the dotted lines extending from line A-B at points 1, 2, 3, 4, 5, 6, 7, 8, and 9. Then at point D, with the radius B-D a quarter circle is drawn (line B&-D&), and this curved line is divided into the same number of parts, namely 10. Then from each point on the curve (n, p, q, r, s, t, u, x, and y), a line parallel to line A-B is drawn to line A-C,[14] where they intersect at points 1, 2, 3, 4, 5, 6, 7, 8, and 9, noticing that point 9 on line A-C is the same distance as point n is from line B&. The same is true with all corresponding points. Then draw a diagonal line from point A to point D and where the line 9-n intersects line

(16) A-D point 10 is established, through that point draw the perpendicular line E-F. Again, where line 8-p intersects the diagonal will mark point 11, through which the perpendicular G-H is drawn. In the same manner, then the line

---

[14] Motta does not indicate these parallel lines on his drawings in Figure VII.

44

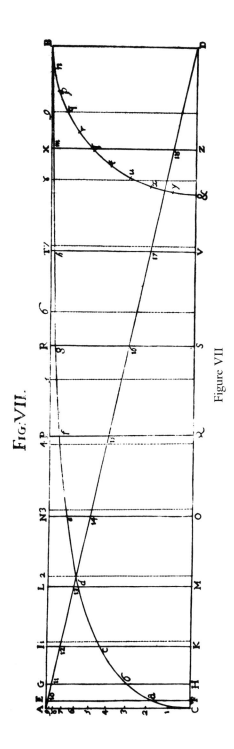

Fig. VII.

Figure VII

45

I-K is determined through points 7-q at 12, line L-M from points 6-r at 13, N-O from points 5-s at 14, line P-Q from points 4-t at 15, R-S from points 3-u at 16, T-V from points 2-x at 17, and X-Z from points 1-y at 18. These perpendiculars will intersect the line A-B at E, G, I, L, N, P, R, T, X, and the points of intersection on these perpendiculars will determine the curvature of the opening, that is to say, if you were to draw a line from point 1 on line A-C and point 1 on line A-B, where they intersect on line E-F will determine point a of the curve; and thus from point 2 to point 2 intersecting G-H at b, points 3 intersect I-K at c, points 4 intersect the line L-M at d, points 5 intersect N-O at e, points 6 at P-Q at f, points 7 through R-S at g, points 8 through T-V at h, and finally points 9 at m. A line is drawn by hand through points a, b, c, d, e, f, g, h, m in such a manner to shape the desired graceful curve because one is not able to draw it perfectly with a compass.

What I have explained to design one-half of the curve applies to the other half as well.

How to Arrange Theatres with *Gradi* or a Single *Palchetto*
Chapter X

For a theatre planned with the symmetry already described, it is then necessary to make it perfect with either *gradi* or *palchetti* so that it will be as commodious for the audience as it is for the Prince. Therefore, we will illustrate both kinds in the plans and side elevations in Figure VIII, which are as follows.

The part of the plan designated as A (in Figure VIII) is for the *gradi* only, which rise to a height of 23 feet above the floor level. The parapet (on which they begin) is 6 feet 4 inches above the auditorium floor and the riser of each row is 19 inches high and the seats are 21 inches wide. The aisle designed as e is 26 inches wide and the riser of the row behind is 28½ inches wide, for reasons explained in Chapter III. The floor or aisle designated as v[15] is 4 feet 6 inches wide and this is wider than aisle e because those who climb the stairs labeled a to this area will descend to the *gradi* from here. This stairway (*a*) is the main one for this half of the auditorium. An identical one is intended for the other side of the theatre. In order to decrease the confusion, it

(17)

---

[15] The v on the plan looks more like a u.

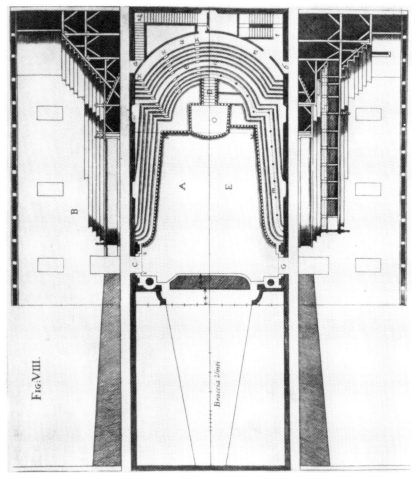

Figure VIII

47

is also possible to include two other stairways that will lead to the aisle *e*.[16] These will serve the people who sit in the *gradi* below aisle e, which divides the commoners from the nobility, making their entrance separate from that of stairway *a*. Stairway *a* will then serve only for the ordinary people who will sit between the two aisles. Thus, there would be four separate entrances for the convenience of filling the *gradi* and consequently clearing them.

In regard to the stairs that lead to the top aisle (v), one is reminded that people descend easier than ascend, in order to avoid any confusion those who assist should not make it difficult to descend, because people always desire the best seats, which are the lowest.

In order to avoid any inconvenience in descending and ascending, especially for the ladies, steps, labeled x, should be located as seen on the plan.

The site O is for the Prince, to which one enters by means of stairway D. His entrance is apart from the others. Site O is enclosed with a balustrade, or whatever else, as shown in the plan, so that in addition to the beauty it provides it conveniently limits its use to those who properly belong there.

I know that many may not be pleased in positioning the aforesaid door C so close to the orchestra, where the people entering can cause a great deal of disturbance and confusion for the performers as well as those in the auditorium. This is especially true when the doors are left unattended. Therefore, on the occasion of the performance, place a corps of guards at the entrances to keep the confusion to a minimum and control the crowds who should not be allowed beyond the dotted line 1-2, where a barrier might be placed. The best remedy is to place a temporary barrier and canopy (or drapery) on the outside of the door.

The width of this theatre is 60 feet and the length 185 feet. I have placed the door C at this location for reasons I have spoken of previously.

Plan B indicates the profile (side elevation), which should be easily understood. It is not necessary to explain how the stage, *proscenio*, and orchestra are arranged, as they are all laid out according to the measurements more on the plan than on the profile.

(18)   Be advised that in all the designs, I show that the seating areas on the sides are contiguous to the smallest proscenium opening, which can very easily be adjusted when the opening is larger.

The plan E in Figure VIII is different from plan A, as it includes one level of *palchetti*. The height from the auditorium floor to the highest seat is 30

---

[16] Motta does not include these stairways in his drawings.

48

feet; this includes a parapet of 6 feet 4 inches, two tiers of seats 3 feet 2 inches high, the *palchetto* 8 feet high, with two rows of *gradi* within the *palchetto*. Above the *palchetto* are two more rows of *gradi* 3 feet 2 inches high, which altogether add up to a height of 30 feet.[17] The width of the level designated as m is double the measurement of the height of a seat and the columns or supports for the level above, with its balustrade, are set in the middle of this space, as can be seen on the dotted line. Another balustrade, the height of the seats, fronts the seats on the level (or floor above the *palchetto*). All this can be seen in the profile or elevation drawing.[18]

All the *gradi* on the main floor and the *piazzette* (aisles) have the same dimensions as indicated for the other plan (A), and the same is true for the site of the Prince.

The top level n is reached by means of the stairway t (which is built in two sections) through the entrance b. From here (m), one enters all the *gradi* above the *palchetto,* which could serve as a private entrance to the *palchetto*.[19] The same is intended for the other half of the plan.

The entrance to the auditorium floor is located at G, and as the others, it should be as commodious as is necessary, as I have observed in my description of plan A.

How Theatres with *Palchetti* Are Constructed

Chapter XI

Two different theatre plans are shown in Figure VIIII, one similar to those already discussed, another different, which illustrates a theatre arranged with levels of *palchetti,* one above the other, but in the form of corridors, as illustrated in profile B for Figure VIIII. The height from the auditorium floor to the top of the third level is 33 feet 6 inches, including the parapet 6 feet 4 inches high, two rows of *gradi* 3 feet 2 inches high, three levels of *palchetti* each 8 feet high, all of which add up to the aforementioned height. The floor above the third level is 6 feet 4 inches wide at its widest width, diminishing proportionately with the angle of the sides. This top level is for the com- (19)

---

[17]The last five rows of *gradi* are in the *loggia*, or rear of the auditorium.

[18]The balustrade for the *gradi* above the *palchetto* is not indicated on the side elevation drawing for plan E.

[19]This stairway is not indicated on plan E.

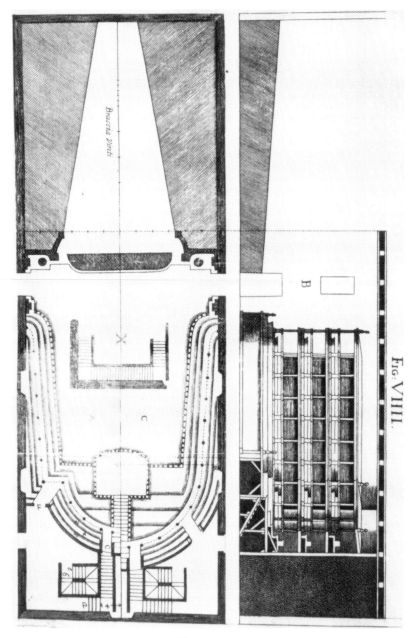

Figure VIIII

moners and a balustrade on the front edge follows the angle of the sides, as indicated.[20] In order that those in the front will not obscure the view of those behind, this upper floor is inclined slightly toward the center of the auditorium, and at least two rows of *gradi* can be placed on this level, making sure that those in front are lower than those behind for the best possible sight lines.

The rows of *gradi* in the *palchetto* are only 35 inches high and the seats only $13\frac{1}{2}$ inches wide so that space can be provided between the *gradi* and the rear wall of the *palchetto* for people to walk through and even stand there, as indicated in row marked 4 on plan A.[21] These seats, as I have said, should be only $13\frac{1}{2}$ inches wide in order to leave the space designated as 3. The floor of this level (corridor) is on the same level as that of the floor in front of the first *grado* (2). The same arrangement is followed in all three levels of *palchetti*.

The stairway that services the two rows of *gradi* on the parapet and the first level of *palchetti* begins at a and ends at c. The steps are 12 inches wide and the risers 6 inches high. The stairs ascend a height of 8 feet 8 inches.

The stairway that services the second level of *palchetti* begins at b and ends at 3, turning twice in its ascent to reach the entrance of the level u. The steps of this stairway are the same as the first and the ascent is 18 feet 3 inches.

Another stairway, indicated by the figure X (not to be compared with the others), leads to the third level of *palchetti*. It begins at M and ends at N, which would be entered through the doorway marked V. The steps of this stairway are 10-$\frac{1}{2}$ inches wide and risers 7-$\frac{1}{2}$ inches high. It ascends 27 feet.[22]

In order to gain access to the seats above the third level of *palchetti*, a small stairway, illustrated by the drawing X (inserted on the auditorium floor of the floor plan), is set directly above the stairway ending at c. Thus, every level of *palchetti* will have its own stairway. The same is intended for the other side of the plan.

The plan C has identical measurements as plan A. For the *gradi* as well as for the *palchetti,* the stairways are identical as in plan A, as indeed are the steps. The only variation in this plan, in any way, is the enlarging the space of the *piazza del theatro* without the side *gradi* converging at angles to the front face of the *piazza del theatro;* namely, making the side *gradi* end along the dotted line 7-8. Then using point 7 as a radius draw the circular form. Each

[20] Not indicated on plan B.
[21] Although not labeled A as indicated in the text, Motta refers to the right side of the floor plan.
[22] Figure VIIII gives no indication of any of the points or where this stairway would be located.

row of *gradi* will join the circular row parallel to the line 7-8. Since the diagram is self-explanatory, there is little need for me to give any lengthy explanation, not even in profile, which would be similar to the profile B in plan A.

(20) How to Arrange a Theatre without a Formal Proscenium Where the Sides Continue to the Same

Chapter XII

This theatre has no formal proscenium arch and the seating on the sides of the auditorium continues to the proscenium wall. The floor plan is similar (so Leon Battista Alberti says in Chapter 7, Book 8) to a form used for the *piede d'un cavallo* (foot ballet). The plan varies, however, in the proportions, as are seen in the plan indicated by ✛ in Figure X. The floor is larger than those I have described, namely, for the operations I have just mentioned. These kinds of theatres are no more impoverished in their majesty than their antecedents because of the lack of a formal proscenium arch. They are excellent indeed for retaining the voice and they are arranged as follows.

Mark off the *occhio della scena* on the line E-F to its greatest width that extends to lines A-B, which includes the position of the orchestra, which is usually 12 feet 6 inches in depth. Then circumscribe a circle as great as the width of the theatre, which will meet tangent to the line A-B at point M. The circle is shown as MNVT. With the center point O, draw the diameter N-T parallel to the line A-B, and with the same center point (O) draw a smaller circle within the large, so that the distance between the two circumferences is 6 feet 4 inches, as indicated by N-X and Z-T. Then draw the diagonals between G-Y and H-L, extending them to intersect the line A-B at points A and B. Then divide the radius O-V in half, which will be point 5, and through this point draw the line 3-4 parallel to the diameter N-T. Then, from points 3 and 4 to A and B, [draw lines] indicated by the dotted lines 3-A and 4-B as well as points A and B to points X and Z, indicated by dotted lines A-X and B-Z. Then form the auditorium floor by the line A, X, 7, Z, B. If you do not wish the sides of the seating area to appear straight, you can give them some curvature by taking one-half of the radius 0-9 and at that point draw the line C-D, and where this line intersects the lines 3-A and 4-B, said

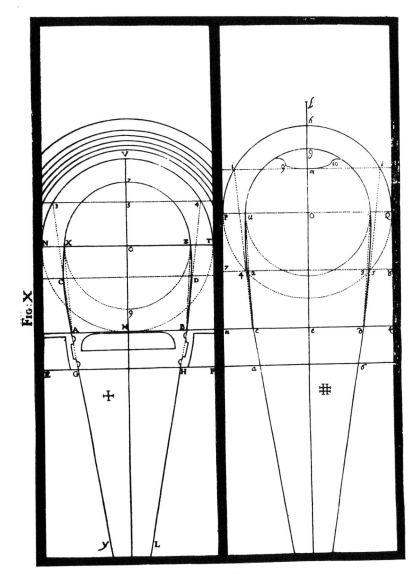

Figure X

53

points C and D will indicate the widest distance of the arcs from the lines X-A and Z-B, which must be drawn by hand.

Since I have shown the height of the *gradi* as well as the *palchetti* in Figures VIII and VIIII, I will not repeat them, as their arrangement is the same. I will only say that when laying out the *gradi,* as in plan A and its profile B of Figure VIII, those *gradi* that occupy the entire width of the theatre (as seen in this diagram by the distance between 7-V), I place these *gradi* beyond point V, as seen in the plan and profile of Figure VIII, mentioned previously. Just so in the present plan, indicated by ❖. The same holds true if one intends to make a theatre with levels of *palchetti,* arranging all the *palchetti* as I have in Figure VIII. The auditorium floor of this plan is 54 feet 3 inches, that is, from points M to 7 and its widest width is 48 feet 3 inches, that is, from X to Z.

(21)

In case you wish an auditorium floor of a greater length, as seen in the plan designated as ❖, you can arrange it as follows: determine the *occhio della scena* A-B and determine the thickness of the opening A-C and B-C. Then indicate the length of the floor as desired, as indicated by E-G, which is 64 feet 6 inches. Beyond the point G the width of the sides is established, which is 1¼ the usual measurements, as indicated by G-H. Then take ½ of the width of the theatre and carry it from the point H toward E through the center point O, which will become the center point to form the two circles, as are indicated in plan ❖, namely, the larger passing through point H and the other through point G. Drawing the line I-L passing through point M, ½ the radius H-O, in order to make the opening C-D of said floor from points I and L, draw lines I-A and L-B, which intersect line N-T and points C and D, at which point these lines are terminated. From said points to V and R, you can draw lines V-C and R-D. When you desire to give the sides a little curvature it can be accomplished in the following manner: divide the lines V-C and R-C in half, that will be at points 2 and 3. Then draw the line 7-8 through these and on this line mark off the distances 7-4 and 8-5, which are equal to the distance G-H. Then divide these distances in half as 4-2 and 3-5, which indicate the widest distance of the arc of lines V-C and R-D, which will form the sides. This rule of proportion will serve to determine the curvature of the sides of a floor of any size. As for the *gradi* or *palchetti,* they are identical to those explained for plan ❖.

The site for the Prince will be arranged along the G-H, or 7-V in plan This can jut out onto the floor space, as seen by the curved line 9-10, passing through point M. The curvature is determined with the radius point

F, which is the same distance beyond point H as is the distance between points G and H. Truly, this form will be the best, not only because of all the adornments that will be applied, but more properly, so that the Prince will be isolated where he may enjoy the admiration of all.

The entrances of doors leading to the auditorium floor are set in the sides, one part of the diameter of the circle in width, toward the stage opening, namely, at points P and Q or N and T on the other plan. How all the others enter and ascend to get to the *gradi* or *palchetti* I have described in the procedures accompanying the foregoing figures.

How to Design Theatres with Divided *Palchetti*

(22)

Chapter XIII

The theatres described this far are designed for Princes and Great Lords in which productions are undertaken solely for the greatest admiration of their magnificence. But there are some theatres, vulgarly called "penny-theatres" because one must not only pay to get in but pay again and again (the manager wanting to make as much profit as possible) to see and hear the spectacle in comfort. I will show ways to design them. It is common practice to design all these theatres with *palchetti* on several levels, the one above the other, but not arranged open as those shown in the elevation drawing in Figure VIIII, but all partitioned, that is, divided one from the other, level by level, each with its individual entrance, rented (as is customary), allowing everyone who uses them the freedom to come and go as they please, without any restrictions and even without being seen.

To make a similar disposition, there are those who have been accustomed to divide or partition the *palchetti* into squares (namely, those on the sides, of which I am speaking), as is indicated by the dotted lines 1-2 in plan X in Figure XI. But dividing them in such a manner is imperfect because only the front spectators can enjoy the scene, while the view of those behind will be cut off because of the incorrect placement of the partitions. And even when they are partitioned diagonally, as indicated by lines 2-4, which are drawn from the center point O, they are still not completely correct. Although this method is better than dividing them into squares, there still are some imperfections. First is the loss of a place in the boxes at the angles marked 2 where no one can sit because of their acuteness. And then people who sit behind

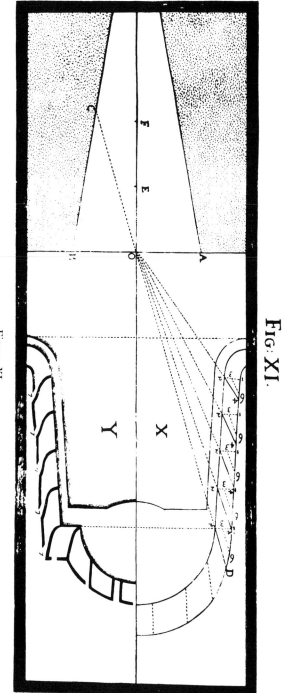

Fig. XI.

Figure XI

56

those in the front will be able to see and enjoy only a part of a scene indicated by OBC, which lines DOC show is less than one-half of the stage. And as the boxes advance closer to the stage they will see even less.

Having made these observations, I will now explain the best way to partition the *palchetti,* as shown by dotted lines 2-3-6, making the straight side 2-3 that amount of space a seated person occupies, that is, between 16 and 18 inches (plan X), which will serve for those in front and constructing the rest of the partition on a diagonal as indicated by the dotted line 3-6, drawing this diagonal not from the center point O but from a point closer to the vanishing point but still in the middle of the opening, as indicated by point E. One could really draw the angle from 6 to the vanishing point, but because the angle would be so acute much would be lost for the aforementioned reasons. The angle generally used is drawn to a point some distance behind the center point O in the middle of the opening as indicated by point F. Thus, even the spectators in the foremost compartments can see the greatest part of the scene. (23)

Because the angles indicated at 3 are obtuse and can become an annoyance (and even cause harm) in entering and leaving the compartments, the partitions can be curved, as shown in plan Y, placing the entrance at the acute angle of the compartment, as indicated by Figure VII. The compartments (or loges) facing the stage are larger than those on the sides and it is possible to make them to accommodate not only two rows of spectators but three and even more when desired. Whatever quality and form I have shown in the present plan, the same ought to be understood in all the other designs in the present work.

The Prince will have his own compartment facing the stage.

The doors and stairways are treated as I have explained in the previous chapter.

How to Decorate Theatres

Chapter XIV

In the arrangement of the various designs shown for the structure of theatres there is nothing to determine how they are to be decorated, nor the expense of a theatre, large or small. The same design may be given the following treatments.

First, one can decorate the theatre with solid ornaments of sculpture, such as cornices, statues, pediments, festoons, columns, balustrades; and other carved relief ornaments with gold and paint.

The second plan is based on the same plan but only those parts that are functional, such as the capitals and cornices, are carved in relief. The rest of the design is painted or highlighted with gold.

The third, following the simple disposition of the *gradi* and *palchetti,* is a more mediocre embellishment. Simply paint all the ornamental elements on their sides for decoration. All of this depends upon the decision of the Prince or Lord who has built it.

Why the Two Doors Are Placed Adjacent to the Orchestra and Some Thoughts on the Wisdom of This Move

Chapter XV

Although some things are done without either reason or purpose, there are many reasons for placing the doors (that is, one on each side), which serve as entrances and exits to the auditorium floor adjacent to the orchestra, as seen in the plan in Figure VIII: first, in order not to disrupt the form of the theatre or its floor; second, because in this position they become a major ornament in the theatre, adjusting their proportions to the stage opening, which one is not able to do with the sides of the *gradi* or *palchetti,* or indeed by putting a door facing the stage, below the site of the Prince; and finally, in order not to lose space along the sides for the crowd. To place an entrance below the Prince is truly very proper but in some cases it is more convenient to place it somewhat higher, that is, on the same level as the floor of the first tier of *gradi,* which is on a higher level than the parapet, placing the steps that serve this entrance someplace else. The best reason for placing the doors adjacent to the orchestra is that it is the closest exit for the crowd in case (God forbid) of fire or any other inconvenience.

The measurements that have served me in the practice of this Art (thanks to opportunities Their Serene Highnesses have provided for me to operate their theatres and the Teatro Fedeli, which I built) are 185 feet by 60 feet. I

(24)

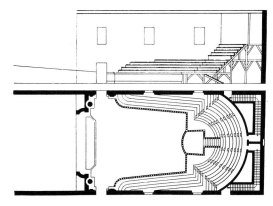

Plan A from Figure VIII

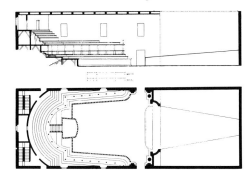

Plan E from Figure VIII

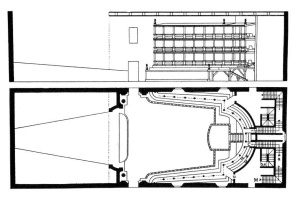

Figure VIIII

Figures VIII and VIIII of the *Trattato,* redrawn by Martin Hammitzsch from *Der Moderne Theaterbau,* vol. 1: *Der Höfische* Theaterbau (Berlin, 1906).

have seen many theatres and in various cities I have observed some practices from which I have formulated a theatre of similar grandeur, with fine proportions, being not too large or too small, but of such a quality in each, particularly at the time of performance, that all are able to see and hear well, even from the greatest distance from the stage. This is the most essential and important of all. Here I have accomplished all I proposed in Chapter X.

I might speak of many other things but inasmuch as my intention has been to describe only the structure, I will omit them now. If I have life I shall not fail to work hard to produce another work in which I will describe the mode of operating these same theatres, showing the designs of various kinds of settings, the arrangement of the substage machinery, how to represent the sea, various things of various worth, and other curiosities in the matter of how to operate the machinery.

The End[23]

[23] Following the conclusion of Chapter XV Motta added the following note to "The Kind Reader": "The Press is like a Circe from which a pen must shift to defend itself like a most skillful Ulysses. Wherefore throughout this essay there are some errors, these are noted here at the end in order not to have to take the time or room with unsatisfactory marginal notes. It is sensible consequently, to add my compliments to you."

This is followed by a list of twelve typographical errors and corrections. The note then concludes with the admonition "Be advised that the letters that I have indicated in the explanation of the figures [in the text] refer to the letters of the ordinary alphabet in the same figures, etc."

Table of Measurements for Auditorium and Stagehouse

A Mantovan *brazza* is 46 centimers or lightly more than 19 inches. An *oncia* is 4 centimeters or approximately 1½ inches. Motta's unit of measurement for large dimensions is 3 *brazza* or approximately 57 inches.

The Auditorium (Figure I, the *Trattato*)

Overall length of auditorium: 117 *brazza* or 185 feet 6 inches

Width of auditorium: 38 *brazza* or 60 feet

Length of the *piazza della scena* (auditorium floor): 44½ *brazza* or 70 feet 6 inches

Width of the *piazza del theatro* ("Place for the Prince"): 19 *brazza* or 30 feet

Depth of the *piazza del theatro:* 8½ *brazza* or 13 feet

Width of the Loggia: 24 *brazza* or 38 feet

Depth of Loggia: 3 *brazza* or 57 inches

Distance between seating on sides of auditorium (*gradi* or *palchetti*) and the proscenium opening: from 4 to 5½ *brazza* or between 6 feet 4 inches and 8 feet 6 inches

Height of parapet (above auditorium floor) on which seating begins: from 3 to 4 *brazza* or between 57 and 76 inches

Gradi (bench seating in continuous rows and tiers):

    Riser: 1 *brazza* or 19 inches

    Seat: 1½ *brazza* or 28½ inches

    Width of aisle in front of first row of *gradi:* from 3 to 3½ *brazza* or between 57 and 66½ inches

    Width of *piazzetta* (aisle in the *gradi*): 3 *brazza* or 57 inches

Palchetti (tiers of open corridors or balconies)

    Height, with *gradi:* 5½ *brazza* or 7 feet

    Height, without *gradi:* 4 brazza or 6 feet 4 inches

    Width of passageway behind *gradi:* 3 *brazza* or 57 inches

Proscenium Opening

Motta does not give any specific measurements except to say that the width of the opening should not exceed 9/12ths of the width of the auditorium and the height should not be any greater than 7/12ths. The difference between the *proscenio* and the *occhio della scena* should not vary more than a unit in width and ½ unit in height within a thickness that does not exceed 2 units. The following measurements are interpolated from Motta's comments on the proscenium opening and the accompanying diagram in Chapter III of the *Trattato*.

  Proscenio (opening on the auditorium side of the wall)
    Width: 9 units (27 *brazza*): 42 feet 9 inches
    Height: 7 units (21 *brazza*): 33 feet 3 inches
  Occhio della scena (opening on the stagehouse side of the auditorium wall)
    Width: 8 units (24 *brazza*): 38 feet
    Height: 6½ units (19½ *brazza*): 31 feet
    Thickness of proscenium opening (depth between *proscenio* and *occhio della scena*) between 57 inches and 8 feet 6 inches

The Orchestra

  The orchestra extends the width of the proscenium opening immediately in front of the stage, projecting out on the auditorium floor 3 to 4 *brazza* or between 57 and 66 inches

The Stagehouse (Figures 1 2 & 3, Plate 1 *Costruzione*)

Length: at least 15 units (45 *brazza*) or 71 feet, 3 inches
Width: at least 15 units (45 *brazza*) or 71 feet, 3 inches [24]
Height at least twice the height of the proscenium opening or approximately 62 feet
Height of stage floor above the auditorium floor (equal to the height of the parapet in the auditorium, upon which the seating begins) 3 or 4 *brazza* or between 57 and 76 inches

[24] Although Motta originally states that the stagehouse should be 15 units wide, he later states that for greater working convenience it is better to add 2 units to each side of the stagehouse bringing his preferred width to 19 units (51 *brazza*), or 90 feet 4 inches. These kinds of inconsistencies make it difficult to give absolutely accurate dimensions in all cases.

Treatise on the structure of theatres and scenes

Ratio of incline of raked stage floor: not less than ⅟20 (1 foot in 20 feet)
  and not more than ⅟16
Substage Area
  Length and width: at least identical dimensions as the stage floor
  Height: at least 4 *brazza* or 6 feet 4 inches
Loft, or "grid," area
  At least as high as the height of the proscenium opening

Costruzione de Teatri,
e
Machine Teatrali
di
Fabrizio Carini Motta Ingeg.r d:
Architetto del Ser.mo Duca di
Mantova 1688.

1773.

Construction of
Theatres & Theatrical Machines

BY

Fabrizio Carini Motta

Engineer & Architect

to

The Serene Duke of Mantova   1688

Unpublished Manuscript

in the

Biblioteca Estense, Modena, Italy

(Item No. Y. C. 316 Campori 979)

[Translation by C. Thomas Ault and Orville K. Larson]

First Discourse on Figure One

On the Proportions of the Stage and the
Symmetry of the Stage
(Plate 1)

Regardless of how concerned with the affairs of the theatre sensitive men are (1) * today, their disregard for the tried and true methods restrict them from representing things onstage properly in regard to both appearance of the settings and the use of stage machinery. Therefore we must continue to find new ways of presenting things naturally, which, so to speak, cannot be represented easily. Audiences are still deprived of seeing what they should see. At best they see only indications. In order to always do the very best productions, it is therefore necessary to lay out and construct the stage, including the areas above and below, in an orderly fashion so that with all due artifice it is possible to represent everything imaginable. But before describing the layout of the stage that must be slotted to allow the chariots that carry the (2) wings to move in these openings, I believe it is of prime importance to consider first the proportions of the stagehouse,[1] which should be as commodious as those of the auditorium, so that everyone who works in it can get along comfortably with his fellow workers. One should not deviate very far from the proportions I set down in my *Treatise on the Structure of Theatres and Scenes.*

In determining the width of the theatre, it is usually divided into twelve units (line A-B of Figure 1 in Plate 1),[2] and on a line perpendicular to this line its length can be determined, which is at least the length of line C-D in Figure 1. The distance between the proscenium opening and the front edge of the orchestra area (C-E) is two and one-half units, and the distance from the orchestra to the leading edges of the *gradi* or *palchetti* (E-F) is one and one-half units. The auditorium floor proper (F-G) is nine units long,[3] not includ-

---

* Numbers in parentheses in the margins indicate page numbers in the original manuscript.

[1] Motta calls the stagehouse the *vaso del teatro,* literally, the "vessel of the theatre."

[2] Although Motta does not say as much, it is obvious that he is recapping here all the dimensions he gives for the auditorium in the third chapter of his *Treatise.* The units of measurement in Figure II of the *Treatise* are identical with those in Figure 1 of Plate 1. The unit is three *brazza,* or approximately 57 inches.

[3] Motta refers here to the opening space between the parapets from which the seating rises. He calls this area the *piazza della scena,* as he does in the *Treatise.*

67

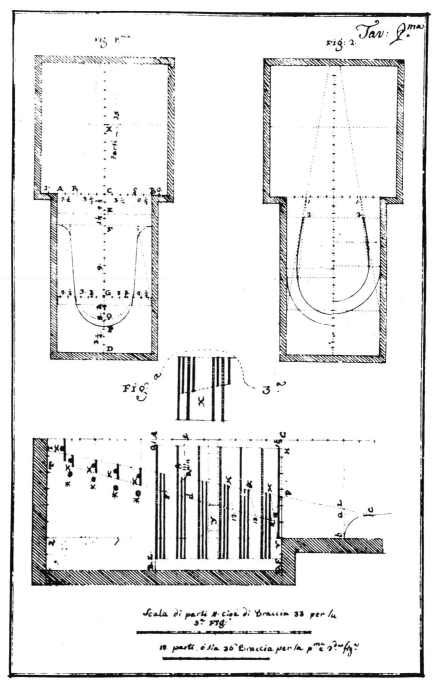

Plate 1. Courtesy of the Comune di Modena and the Biblioteca Estence.

ing the circular area at the rear of the auditorium. The radius of the curvature of the front ends of *gradi* or *palchetti* is either one and two-thirds units (L-M), or two and one-quarter (F-L).[4]

The circular area H-G with center point G forms the *piazza del teatro,* which joins the *gradi* or *palchetti* at points H-O.[5] The stagehouse should extend four units beyond each side of the proscenium opening to ensure the best working space. Also, for convenience, the depth of the stagehouse should be no less than fifteen units. However, when it is deeper it can produce great vistas of extreme depth. (3)

The parts of the stage designated for the chariots and the borders above should occupy an area eight units deep (line C-X of Figure 1) of the stagehouse in which the arrangement of the chariots will be explained later. The auditorium ceiling should be ten units above the stage and the proscenium opening six units high. As for the construction of the *gradi* or *palchetti,* the proscenium, the orchestra or other items, their construction is governed by the instructions in the aforementioned *Treatise on the Structure of Theatres and Scenes.*[6]

Second Discourse on Figure Two

(Plate 1)

In addition, I do not wish to omit instructions on how to establish the parts of theatres that do not have a formal proscenium arch. It is the same with large or small *piazza della scena.* If you follow Figure 2, which I hope is self-explanatory, it is not necessary for me to say more than that the distance 1-1 is the width of the proscenium, 1-2 the depth of the orchestra, and at points 2 the *gradi* or *palchetti* begin.

---

[4] Motta's drawing (Figure 1), however, does not include the letters L-M or F-M. In reality, Motta is talking about the left side of the stage when he refers to the letters L-M and to the right side when he refers to the letters F-M.

[5] Motta fails to label the points H and O on his drawing, but obviously they are the diameter of the circular area along the line G.

[6] All of these measurements may be found in the Table of Measurements that follows the translation of the *Trattato.*

Third Discourse on Third Figure
On the Construction of the Stage,
Divided for the Movable Wings
(Plate 1)

(4)   Stages have always been constructed in various ways, according to the ca-
prices of the stage machinists and "professors of this art" who have tried
every way under the sun to make the chariots and other slotted items work
conveniently. It is not my intention to insinuate which method is best, but I
shall describe and illustrate a procedure that will serve for all operations
without having at times to eliminate some part or having to design another,
all of which can cause much trouble later. Not only is this always a burden-
some procedure for whoever is involved, but it makes it very difficult to
maintain any procedural uniformity. To explain and make myself more easily
understood, I have drawn two plans: one iconographic, representing the
floor plan of the stagehouse, and the other sciographic, representing a section of the stage.

   The stagehouse is divided into two parts as seen in Plate 1, showing the
distribution of the eight parts assigned to the wing-chariot system, as illustrated by the section of the plan labeled ABCD in Figure 3 of Plate 1, which
represents one-half of the stage floor. To lay out the aforementioned grooves
(5)   and streets it is first necessary to know that the unit of measurement for each
unit in these drawings is 57 inches. Thus, the functional width of the auditorium will be 57 feet and the stagehouse 47 feet 6 inches.

   The eight parts A-C are 38 feet deep in which six sets of slots and streets
will be laid out. Each street is 3 feet 9 inches wide and each set of slots 30
inches. Each set of slots consists of three openings in the stage floor 3 inches
wide with a 9-inch space between the slots. Thus, each set of slots is laid out
within the prescribed eight sections, that is, 38 feet in depth. The 9-inch
spaces between the three slots are necessary so that the chariots carrying the
wings will have sufficient space to move back and forth the allotted distance
without any concern that they will foul one another, as they often leap because of the change of speed, or because of the great force generated as they
accelerate, causing them to rise out of plumb. When the circumstances pro-
hibit sufficient space to travel smoothly, they jam into the chariots ahead
causing great confusion and inconvenience. This I have seen happen too
many times. The wider spaces are also advantageous because many times the

wings are hung double on the chariots, one in front of the other, which is removed for another scene.

The sets of slots do not extend to the side walls of the stagehouse but stop 38 inches short—thus providing a passageway between them and the wall, as (6) indicated by E-F on the drawing. The last slot of each set extends onstage almost to the center on a slightly diagonal line. The exact distance from the center is 19 inches at point G and 28 inches at point H. The other slots of each set (whose chariots I shall call laterals) will not extend any farther on-stage than is indicated by line I-L.

To find the width of the side wings, extend a perpendicular line from point b where the curved front end of the *gradi* or *palchetti* joins the side wall of the auditorium. On line b-a determine the radius (b-a) that swings from point a and intersects the front edge of the *gradi* or *palchetti* at point c. Thus, the distance from b-a is equal to a-c. The same procedure is used on the opposite side. Then, from point c extend a line through P (the side edge of the proscenium opening) to point I on the rear wall. The dotted line P-I indicates the onstage edge of each wing in each successive set of slots as they recede to the rear of the stage. Next, establish point x offstage from M along the line of the first slot in the first set of chariots. Then, using the distance P-x as a radius, swing an arc from point R that intersects the first slot of the last set of slots at S. Then draw a line from x through S that extends back-stage to where it intersects the rear wall of the stagehouse at T. The line xST will indicate the offstage edge of each wing in each set of slots.

The *prospettiva* can close off the scene at every set of slots. The *prospettiva* is (7) divided into four frames, that is, two on a side, for the greater convenience in both handling and masking. The width of these is found in the following manner:[7] the line d-e is divided equally, the center of which is indicated at point g. Then along the same line points u and n are established 4½ inches on each side of point g.[8] Thus, the width of the two frames on one side of the *prospettiva* will be d-n and u-e. The frame u-e, which is carried on the chariot in the rear slot of the set that extends onstage to the exact center, as indicated on line G-H and the frame d-n, is hung on one of the other

[7] Motta uses the first slot of the fifth set of chariots in his explanation, when in reality he should have used the second or third. The small letter g that indicates the center of line d-e is somewhat obscured as it is placed in the heavy line of the third slot.

[8] Motta's explanation is that the overall distance between r and n is 4½ inches with point g as the center. The literal translation of Motta's explanations in this discourse is extremely terse and obscure; therefore, a certain amount of extrapolation based on Figure 3 in Plate 1 (in which the letters of the text do not always correspond to those in the drawing) enters into the translation of these explanations.

chariots as the imagination demands. The onstage edge of the front frame overlaps the rear frame the distance between u and n (when their edges are in view). Thus, the observer's eye does not pass between the frames and the two frames d-g and g-e appear as a single unit. The same operation can be performed in the last set of slots, arranging the frames on the chariots as described. In this way, the slots that extend onstage to line G-H, besides whatever other convenience they may provide, can close the scene at each set of slots, increasing or decreasing the depth of the scenes as may be required.

(8)   They [chariots] are also used to bring individual pieces of scenery, such as columns, statues, trees, and similar items, onstage. For these effects I have also indicated slot H-V, which is of great convenience.

The wings set behind the wing-chariots are arranged according to the width of the scene, large or small. They are set up more or less as wings are usually arranged.

One should always take the trouble to leave a passageway behind the *prospettiva* so that it is easy to move things behind the scene and also to allow people to cross-over backstage while a scene is open. Such a passageway is not unusual, it is a part of all backstage areas.

The scene is never closed in the first set of slots or before them. It is not good to close the scene at such a short distance from the spectators.

When the stage is not as deep as the one presently described, a lesser number of grooves are needed. And then four slots are desired in the last two sets of chariots, two of these will extend onstage as far as line P-I and the other two as far as line G-H so that two sets of *prospettiva* may be used to close off the scenes in these longer slots, as shown in slots x-9.[9]

In the larger backstage area, all the streets are 45 inches wide. Each slot is approximately 3 inches wide and the spaces between the slots in the first four sets are approximately 8½ inches wide and approximately 9½ inches between the last two sets. This arrangement will be the most convenient (Figure a- - ⁻ - - 3a in Plate 1).

In the case when the stage and stagehouse are the same width and are narrower than the width of the auditorium, as indicated by line V-Z, it is necessary to arrange the first two slots of the first three sets of chariots diagonally, as shown by the dotted lines M-V, &-13, and 12-K. When they are laid out in this fashion not without some difficulty, less space is required to close

---

[9] Motta refers here to the smaller diagram marked X (Figure a -⁻--- 3a in Plate 1) showing the arrangement of two sets of chariots with four slots in each set, two of which extend to the center of the stage. The numeral 9, to which Motta refers, is not indicated.

the scenes. When they are arranged thus, on the diagonal to conserve space and also for the convenience of masking the wings (including the wings of the first set, which will be set very close), the arrangement consequently is very manageable, as M-14 indicates. The remaining sets of slots may be left parallel.

When the stagehouse is less than 47 feet 6 inches deep, the slotted section of the stage will occupy only 30 feet of the depth of the stage, which may be divided in the following manner. Only five sets of chariots are necessary on such a stage, and these according to two arrangements. First, three sets of (10) three slots and two with four. Or four sets of three slots and the last set of four. In the first arrangement the width of the streets between the sets of slots is 39½ inches, the width of the slots 3 inches, and the spaces between the slots 8½ inches. In the second plan, the width of the streets is 42 inches, the width of the slots the same, and the spaces between the slots 9 inches. When the width of the stage is the same as the width of the stagehouse, as shown by line V-Z, the divisions set forth above will work in this space.

It is also possible to construct a smaller theatre whose stagehouse is only 38 feet deep. Each of the eight divisions allotted to the slotted portion of this stage floor will be 38 inches. Consequently, the eight divisions will occupy 25 feet 3 inches, to be divided as follows: the first street will be 38 inches wide and the other four 40 inches. The space between the slots are only 2¼ inches wide because in this smaller theatre the chariots, which will support the smaller frames, will also be smaller in construction. When it is necessary to close the scene farther downstage, it may be done in front of the other sets of grooves, as I have described.

In these smaller theatres it is possible to arrange the *prospettiva* with only two frames, one on each side, if they are not too large and do not jam the wings. I think it best, however, to use four frames as in a larger theatre, al- (11) though the space is lacking to facilitate the work and movement in the smaller theatre, because even though the frames are small and much easier to be handled or carried by anyone, as beneficial as this may be in the small the-atre, these frames will not represent (proportionately) what is seen on the larger stage.

When, however, the stagehouse is even deeper than those already dis-cussed, perhaps as much as 67 feet, which is truly a considerable depth in which large crowds can be accommodated, and which is very adequate for any kind of a large theatre, enabling the public to see and hear easily (if it is larger, hearing becomes more difficult). Each division will be 5 feet 8½ inches. The eight allotted to the space for the chariots will total 45 feet 6 inches. The distribution includes seven sets of grooves and seven streets. All streets are 45 inches wide. The first four sets of grooves have three slots each, the fifth four slots, the sixth three, and the seventh or last four. Each slot is the usual width of 3 inches. The space between the slots of the first three orders 9 inches and the spaces between the remaining four 8½ inches. In this way the eight parts of the grooved portion of the stage will encompass 44 feet, 4 inches.

(12)   I do not advocate making the streets wider than those I have used in small stages, nor any narrower than those for a stagehouse of 65 feet. First, that is a wide enough street. Also, it does not require that the frames have to be so wide; for having to make them very wide, the very strong timbers necessary (considering their width and height) will make them very heavy and difficult to handle. This creates difficult shifting problems onstage, when one considers the very large number of wings one has on hand necessary to create the various scenes.

    Between one order of wings and another, that is, in the street areas of the stage, the floor is completely trapped. These traps extend completely from one side to the other, as indicated by line E-F (which extends to the other side). These traps should not exceed between 5 feet 6 inches and 8 feet in width so that they can be lowered and closed easily, as indicated by the dotted sections in the street labeled Y. The traps are hinged from below and are held shut with chains. Traps are used in all streets except those immediately in front of and behind the first set of grooves, because the stage floor of the

(13)   first and second streets must be built very solid to support the dancers and all others who work on the stage. Also, apparitions are almost never created so close to the audience. Here are some requirements for these traps. The traps are attached from below and not to the front, so that when they hang open the trapdoors themselves mask the vision of the people in the orchestra and the *gradi* from seeing below stage, which will not happen when they are attached to the front.

Fourth Discourse on the Fourth Figure
Elevation of the Stage
(Plate 2)

The sciographic drawing (Figure 4a), representing the side elevation of the stage, illustrates the method of arranging the large main timbers or beams that are located between the slots and the streets. The timbers between the slots are wide. The measurements I have given indicate the distances between the slots AB and CD, which are included as a part of the street.[10] A narrower width of 6 inches may be used, which would allow for a wider trap. Although the beams can be as wide as desired, 6 inches is sufficient. The drawing illustrates one set of four slots for the *prospettiva* and another with three. (14)

The main beams should be long enough to extend from one side wall of the stagehouse to the other (indicated as I), securely fastened beneath the stage so they will remain solidly in place.

The scaffolding is supported from the ground, built upon the oak beams (E), which are set on the stone pylons (F). The latter are built so that the edges extend slightly beyond the beams, as indicated as z-3, in order to support the traps between the pylons. When the traps are closed, they facilitate the coming and going (onstage) and they can be opened to accommodate storage in the subterranean areas between the pylons.

It is necessary that the substage area as well as the slotted stage floor be kept clear as possible for the various machines as well as for changing the scenery. Too much clutter interferes with the chariots, poles, ropes, and other paraphernalia necessary to operate them.

On the floor, 3, 4, 5, 6, which is called the substage area, the chariots should run in their tracks as indicated as d. I place the traps (e), which close the subterranean area, lower than the substage floor on which the chariots move for a greater convenience in their use. The traps extend between the pylons and they are not as inconvenient as they would be if they were set in the substage floor as indicated between points 4 and 5. (15)

---

[10] Motta's statements require some explanation. His phrase "which are included as a part of the street" obviously refers to the fact that the width of beams B and C (in Figure 4a) are included in the overall measurement of the width of the street between the two sets of slots AB and CD. His next statement, "a narrower width of 6 inches may be used, which would allow for a wider trap" refers to the fact that the "streets" between the sets of slots are trapped to allow scenery to be lowered and raised (see discourse 19). A narrower beam on each side of a set of slots obviously would allow for a wider trap. Actually, on his drawing Motta indicates the wider beam between the slots for each set of chariots, while the end beams A-B-C-D indicate the narrower beams to which Motta refers.

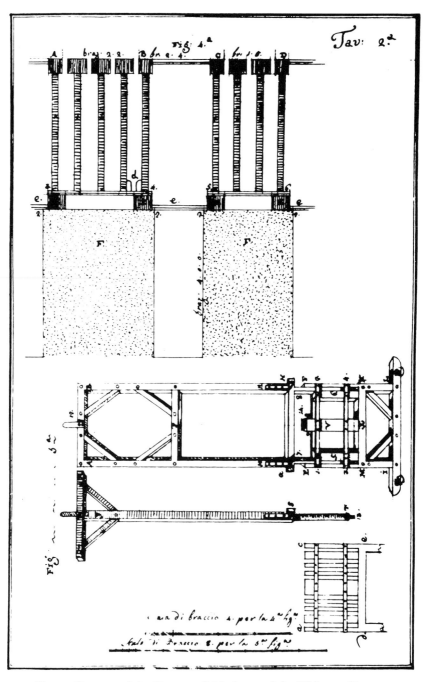

Plate 2. Courtesy of the Comune di Modena and the Biblioteca Estence.

Below stage along the side walls a passageway 38 inches wide is provided at each end of the chariots, which corresponds to an identical passageway on the stage floor above, as labeled E and F in Figure 3, on the same level as the subterranean traps, thus leaving the tracks on which the chariots move elevated above said floor.

The substage area should be at least deep enough so that one can walk upright along the passageway, which is to say the overall height should be 6 feet 4 inches, not including the thickness of the beams.

Fifth Discourse
On Chariots—Fifth Figure
(Plate 2)

After the stage has been constructed, as I have explained, it is necessary to create the scenery for it. So many inventions are used, such as triangles on pivots, wings, or as is commonly stated, "according to the book." Although these pivoting pieces and various other methods are common, the current custom is to use wings traveling on what are called "guides," as the wings are guided by them. These guides are set perpendicular in slots in the stage floor from the substage below, and they move out across the stage as is necessary, holding the painted wings firm and secure.

This method of making the scenes appear with the aforementioned "guides" is the most convenient ever devised, not only because they do not foul up onstage but also because they provide the diversity today's operations assume. (16)

I know that it is usual to build the chariots all in one piece according to their heights. However, for the convenience of which I shall speak presently, I deem it best, even necessary, to construct these chariots in two sections. One is the section onstage called the guide to which the wings are attached; the other, which works on the substage below, is the cart that carries the guide, to which the guide is easily joined, as indicated by ABCD in the drawings (5a in Plate 2).

The part indicated as ECFD is the cart below stage and AGBH as the guide to which the wings onstage are attached. The height of the carts will be determined by their substage location, since the further upstage they are located (below stage), the taller each receding set must be because of the rake of the stage floor above. However, regardless of its height, the height of sec-

77

tion ENFN of each cart remains constant, which should not be less than 47 inches.

(17)   The posts E-I and F-L form the sides of the frame of the cart at each end of the crossbeam M-N. The frame is constructed of strong, joined timbers, as indicated by 1, 2, 3, 4 on the diagram. Inside the frame at the end posts E-N and F-M, the boards 5 and 6 are set parallel to the posts thus forming a shaft into which posts 7 and 8 slide, joining the guide to the cart, uniting the two parts into a unified whole.

The posts 7 and 8 are simply there to join the guide to the cart; however, they are cut opposite to those of the cart. The protruding side edges of these shafts E and F move through the slots of the stage floor grooves and they extend up only to the level, but never above, the stage floor. Sliding between the beams of the slots, they thus regulate the cart and guide, holding them both perpendicular as they move through the slots. A horizontal iron band 1-2 is placed on each cart just below the bottom edge of the slot beam. The distance between the substage cart track to the top edge of the stage floor determines the overall height of each set of carts.

(18)   The guides themselves A-G-B-H are all constructed the same height. This measurement is determined by the necessary height of the last order of wings, as indicated at A in Figure 3. These guides must be 9 inches shorter than the wings of the last order, and horizontal rail P is set at least 6 feet above the bottom guide beam G-H. The guide frame is strengthened with diagonal braces, as indicated on the drawings. I have left the area below the horizontal rail P open, so that if an opening is necessary in the painted wings, there will be no obstructions in the guide frame.

The bottom beam of the cart C-D runs along the track on the substage floor, directly beneath the slots. The ends of the beam 1-C and L-D, which contain the two wheels that facilitate the movement, should be proportionately wide and strong enough to support the size of the cart so that it will always run smoothly. However, they should never be less than 16 inches long.

Iron hooks 10 and 11 are riveted to the guideposts G and H to carry the wings. Similarly, the wings are securely fastened at 12 on the top rail A-B, to hold them straight by means of spiking a horizontal rail, at a similar level in the wing, to the rail A-B of the guide. Therefore, to securely fasten them to the guide, the wings are attached to the posts A-G and B-H on the sides with hooks, that is, one per post at the height G-H, which a man standing on the stage floor can easily reach, which is between 66 and 76 inches. All the

(19)   wings are similarly fitted with eye-rings at the same height, which fit over the hooks.

Construction of theatres and theatrical machines

It will be observed that when the wings are constructed, each will have a horizontal rail at the appropriate height in which the eye-rings are fastened so that the wings can be easily hung on the hooks on the guides.

Because the variety of operations are so numerous and they must be carried out in view of the audience in various ways, I have also created another type of guide point, Q, R, S, T. This one is the same height as the others and is moved in the same type of cart. It sets between the iron straps or horizontal rail 1-2 into a shaft labeled V that extends up to the stage-floor level, identically to the cart ends E and F. This shaft is circular in shape, and in the beam that supports it at the bottom a smaller hole is drilled, so that the tip of the guide pole (13), which is also a smaller diameter than the shaft, will fit into it snugly, thus stabilizing the rotating main pole as it turns when it carries a boat. To make the guide pole immobile, a bolt is passed through the shaft at 14 (above V). This also helps to ensure the rigidity of the top spar of the guide pole AR, so that it will not turn and jam on some obstruction. This guide is easily carried and managed onstage.

Similarly, the posts on this T-guide will be fitted with iron hooks: one (20) below and two above to support the wings. They are attached to the post by means of iron bands set in notches in the beam. Individual wings are easily mounted to the post Y.S with a pin that secures the iron bands and always stays with the post.

For greater convenience in changing scenery, the carts used in the slots that extend to the center of the stage, as indicated along line G-H in Figure 3, are constructed according to the diagram a, c, d, e in Figure 5, which is similar to the cart EFMN, except that two more supports are added and spaced so that three openings 3½ inches wide are created, as indicated in diagram a, (21) c, d, e. These spaces serve as additional shafts to be used as necessary when these carts are used to carry isolated columns, trees, statues, fountains, and similar items onstage. They work together, or separately, moving all the way to center stage, or off to the side, depending on the type of cart used and what is being presented.

The reason for making the height of all guides, as well as the posts and shafts, one uniform size is for convenience. If each individual cart had its own particular guide, that would only add to the confusion during the haste of shifting settings. Those who do the work deserve some consideration: to avoid losing time during changes looking for the first, second, or third guide when they are not identical only makes it more difficult. It is easier to make them all the same, so any guide will work in any cart. This is a very good and simple operation.

Sixth Discourse

How to Illuminate the Stage—Sixth Figure

(Plate 3)

(22) I have used various methods of lighting the stage, both movable and stationary, and I have found some difficulties in all of them, for the obstructions they create are just as great as the inconveniences in moving them. For this reason, I advocate the following method, which I believe is very good as well as easy to perform by those who change the wings.

After the stage has been constructed as described in the third discourse, holes must be drilled through the upstage beam of the third slot of each set of slots, holes that reach down through the beam into the supporting posts 19 inches deep set under the beam from the substage floor below, as shown in diagram G. These holes are placed between the space A-B, indicating the onstage edge of the slots, and C-D, indicating the offstage edge, as shown in drawing 6a. I suggest three positions in each beam, as indicated by 1, 2, 3, in beam E.[11] The third position, however, does not need any post below, as it is close enough to the end of the beam that is fastened into the side wall of the stagehouse to make further support unnecessary. The apparatus to provide

(23) the light, as shown by Figure H, consists of the wooden frame 6, 7, 8, 9 attached to the pole 4-5; this vertical unit is used to provide the brilliant illumination. It is lined with tin to prevent the light from shining through the wings as well as providing protection from fire. The bottom end of the pole (5), which extends below the frame, is inserted in the holes in the beam. Position 1 should be far enough behind line A-B so that it will always be concealed by the wings during scene changes. The pole or armature of the light unit that fits into the holes in the beam is long enough that the unit sets 8 inches above the beam.

Figure 10-11 illustrates the batten 10-14-11 (in diagram 6) used to fasten the support post (5) to the main beam, as indicated at 12-13 on line C-A, in order to keep the post solid and immobile. This board should extend up the side of the beam only as much as is necessary to fasten it securely to the beam.

(24) After the light unit is constructed, as many brackets (as illustrated by drawing L) as necessary to hold the torches and the candles are inserted in

---

[11]The beam is not labeled in the drawing; however, positions 1, 2, and 7 are indicated along line C-A.

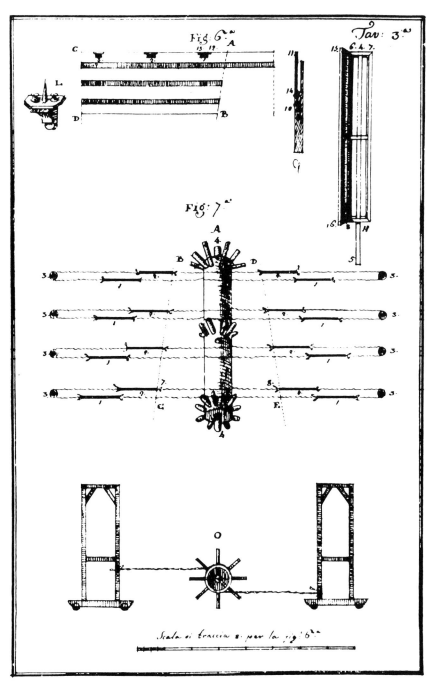

Plate 3. Courtesy of the Comune di Modena and the Biblioteca Estence.

the unit. However, when candles are used, more brackets are necessary. Thus, it is possible to move the light unit from position 1 to 2 or 3 when it is necessary to enlarge the scene, or when it is necessary to represent night, because when the lights are moved to the sides the center of the stage becomes darker. The units may be moved, however, for whatever reasons necessary.

These lights may also be made to turn in positions 1, 2, or 3 when rounded shafts are used. They can turn to represent night and make the stage darker by turning the open part of the unit toward the wall. Thus, it is best to line the back (15-16) as well as the sides of unit with tin so it will reflect the light when day is represented as well as for better concealment when night is desired by rotating them, as has been described.

(25)

Seventh Discourse on the Seventh Figure
On the Arrangement for Scene Changes
(Plate 3)

Various arrangements for the chariots that move the wings into the view of the audience are customary, and it is quite true that the majority of them use a drum located beneath the stage that "runs" longitudinally between the chariots, and its length is determined by the number of sets of chariots and slots. I rig all the ropes necessary to move the chariots on this drum; and according to the opinion of other machinists I vary the methods of making it revolve for those spectators who want the quickest changes, scarcely perceived, as well as for those who enjoy seeing the operation of this ingenious art. Therefore, since this is the case, it is essential to show the customary methods as well as other innovations to understand the complexity of this art.

(26)

One of the arrangements is indicated in Figure 7 at A. The chariots are all labeled 1 and 2. Four sets are shown and it is understood that they all move only as far onstage in their slots as indicated by lines B-C and D-E on the drawing. All of these are rigged to the drum G. Permanent lines are attached from the onstage edge of the chariots (2) to the drum, and enough rope attached from the other chariots (1) to drum as is necessary to move the chariots on and offstage. This is illustrated in the drawing; for the rope for chariot 7 is passed over the top and around the drum, while the rope for chariot 8 is passed around the drum from the bottom. The offstage chariots

(1) have their ropes attached to the drum in just the opposite manner, that is to say, when the chariots onstage are rigged from below the drum, those offstage are rigged across the top of the drum. Then, the offstage ends of the two chariots in the same set (1 & 2) are connected with another rope that is threaded through the pulley 3, which is set in a fixed position as is indicated in the drawings.

The diameter of the drum should be equal to the distance from the center (27) of one chariot (1) to the center of the other (2), as seen at 6a g, so that the ropes will pull straight.[12]

The ends of the drum are capped (closed) with round discs approximately 28½ inches in diameter that revolve on the shaft (4), and these discs are fitted with strong wooden spokes that extend beyond their edges. The men will turn the drum by means of these wooden arms when a new scene must be brought into view and the old one "happily withdrawn." With a little thought this is all easily understood.

This method of changing scenes is quick when the stagehands are very strong. Also, the larger the diameter of the drum, the faster the change, although it will require more force to turn.

As illustrated in the drawing O, the ropes that are attached permanently from the chariots to the drum will always be attached to the lines that are always parallel to the substage floor. Hence, those that run above and over the drum will be attached at one height, and those that run around from below will be attached at the lower height. (28)

The sets of chariots are arranged so that when one set is onstage the offstage set is dressed in order that no opening occurs between the wings allowing the spectators to see through the wings.

The importance of the procedures just explained cannot be overemphasized because they are procedures that should be followed whenever drums are used.

Seventh Discourse on Figure Seven[a]

(Plate 4)

The design H is the same arrangement as indicated in Drawing A (on the previous plate) and does not differ in any way with the exception that instead of using the wooden arms to move the drum, a double sheave is placed in the

---

[12] 6a g is not indicated in diagram 7.

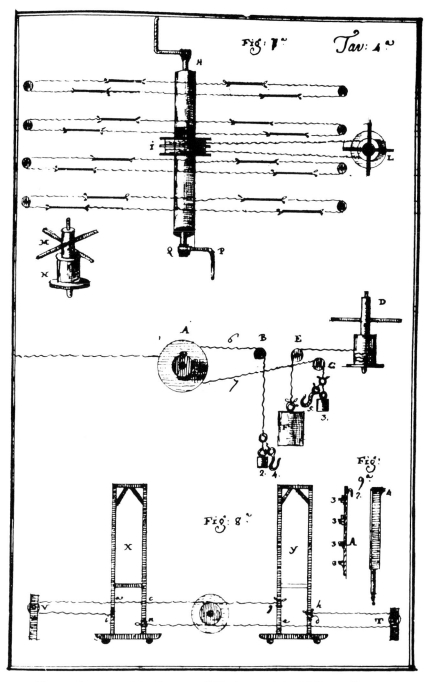

Plate 4. Courtesy of the Comune di Modena and the Biblioteca Estence.

center of it. Two large ropes called course lines or cables wound opposite to each other are rigged from these sheaves to a capstan (L), which is set at a right angle to the drum. The ropes are so arranged that as the drum and capstan turn, the rope from one sheave unravels as it is rolled onto the capstan, as the second rope from the capstan unravels as it rolls onto the second sheave in the drum. The cord lines are just long enough to move the chariots on and offstage and they run from the sheaves I to the capstan L parallel to the substage floor.

The drum may be constructed of any desired diameter and the same is true (29) of the double sheave. However, the diameters should take into account the length of the drum, and it should be of sufficient strength so its axle will not bend. The larger the double sheaves are, the lesser the force that is necessary to make the drum revolve. However, the chariots will always move slower (than the previous method), and even slower when the diameter of the capstan is small. Hence, there is an inviolable rule: the more the force is reduced, the slower the movement will be proportionately, and conversely as the force is increased, proportionately, the movement will be accelerated as demonstrated by mechanics. Accordingly, when the double sheaves can be made one-half diameter larger than that of both the capstan and drum, and the spokes of the capstan are four times the length of the diameter of the capstan, a very quick change can be achieved as one and one-half turns of the capstan will turn the drum one complete revolution.

The drawing M shows the height of the capstan L, and the disc N holds the cables in place, keeping them from slipping off, which would impede the movement of the capstan.

In small theatres where the size of the chariots and wings are necessarily (30) smaller, with subsequently less weight, the drum can be turned by fastening cranks and handles on each end of the axle of the drum. The cranks are set opposite to one another as seen at Q-P and turned by the stagehands. The scene changes as the drum is turned and the distance the chariots move is in direct relationship to the force created, due to the length of the crank handles P-Q.

Be advised that I assume my readers are familiar with backstage practices and equipment such as drums, axles, capstans, winches, sheaves, sockets, pulleys, shafts, pins, planes, cables, ropes, course lines, fouled-up lines, etc., as well as materials such as timber, for if I happen to omit the description or operation of some things that I should have, they can be figured out in accordance with the operation under discussion.

Figure Seven in the Fourth Plate
(Plate 4)

In order to effect rapid scene changes, instead of the cable arrangement with the double sheaves and capstan, which I have just illustrated in H (Figure 7), a counterweight, heavy enough to turn the drum, is attached to it by means (31) of two cables. These cables are rigged so that one cable can turn the drum one way and another, the other, thus regulating the operation according to which chariots must move onstage.

A winch is placed above in order to raise the fallen counterweight, to attach it to the lines that operate the drum. The arrangement is illustrated in this drawing. The drum is labeled P and the double sheave is labeled A. Attached to these are the cables 6 & 7, which are threaded through the pulleys B & C. Hooks, 4 & 5, are permanently attached to the ends of these cables, as well as the small weights 2 & 3, whose sole purpose is to keep these lines taut when loose. The hooks, 4 & 5, are large and strong enough to carry the counterweight F when it is hooked onto them. The counterweight F, in turn, is permanently attached to the winch D with another cable. To operate, the weight is attached to one of the cables 6 or 7. Using cable 7 as an example, it is securely locked onto counterweight 7 above, and when the counterweight is released to fall, the drum, as it is turned by the unwinding cable 7 to change the scene, simultaneously rewinds the hanging line 6, raising it up to the height of the winch. Thus, for the next scene change, the counterweight is unhooked from the extended line 7 below, raised up to the position of the winch where it is then hooked onto cable 6. When the weight is released, the operation is repeated, however, turning the drum in the opposite direction.

(32) The operation must be arranged and regulated with great care. The pulleys B, C, E that support the cables must be so placed that the operation works smoothly, and so that when the chariots are all in place and set to move, the lines will not snap due to the weight of the counterweight F.

Eighth Discourse on the Eighth Figure
Another Method Very Convenient for
Rigging the Chariots
(Plate 4)

One can see how convenient, as well as necessary, the drums with sheaves are. Now, I would like to explain how one can also use two. One regulates the first set of chariots in each order, and the other operates the second. These never move further onstage than the line B-C (in Figure 7a), as can the third order. These two drums are located in the center of the substage area and they run absolutely parallel to the sides of the stagehouse, as previously explained, and they are rigged as shown in Figure 8ᵃ.

The permanent lines n and q, attached to the front edges of the chariots X and Y, are rigged to the drum P with the line q turned over the top and the line n turned up from below. Then the line i and h are threaded through the pulleys V and T, which I have already explained are not on the same level but one above the other. Line h passes through holes e, d drilled in the supports of chariot Y and are rigged around the drum P from the bottom, and line i passes through holes a, c drilled in the supports of chariot X and are wrapped around the drum from below, both with enough rope to accommodate the operation. (33)

This method is very convenient because not only is there freedom to move the first set of chariots without moving the second, but by dividing the weight in half, the manpower to move each drum is decreased. By setting the pulleys one above the other, and running the lines through the chariots, the lines are always controlled and there is no danger of the lines slipping into the tracks beneath the chariots, which frequently happened when the lines are all set on the same level, and they are stretched from the heat and are set in motion by the air.

The capstans should be placed on the sides, one for each drum, in straight alignment to the sheave on the drum, rigging the lines as I have explained, placed where there cannot be any possible obstructions. These drums may be used for whatever and whenever necessary. This arrangement is the very best, as two drums make the operation that much easier.

Ninth Discourse on the Ninth Figure
How to Make Scene Changes with Only
One Order of Chariots
(Plate 4)

(34)   I have explained how to use two drums, employing one for the first order of chariots and another for the other. Now I wish to explain how to work with only the first order of chariots, which is the one in front, without using the second except to utilize their carts, which remain stationary.

Instead, the T-guides are used. I have already explained how they are constructed and how they are inserted into the chariots onto which the wings are mounted.

Having set the wings for the first scene on the first order of chariots out
(35)   onstage in view of the audience, the wings for the next scene are mounted on the previously mentioned T-guides in the stationary chariots in the second slots, directly behind the wings mounted for the first scene. However, they must remain hidden behind the wings of the first order of chariots. To make the change, the first order of chariots is moved offstage, revealing the wings set on the T-guides. Then the withdrawn wings are removed and another scene set on the first set, which can be moved back onstage in front of the scene mounted on the stationary T-guides. The operation is easy, and there is nothing else to explain except to mention that the wings on the first set of chariots must always be large enough to conceal those behind.

Then, when one wants to create a very wide scene, much wider than usual, the carts and the T-guides are moved farther offstage. However, in this case, they must be moved by means of the drum, but they are maneuvered easily with the capstan.

Similarly, the T-guides are used for the wings in the perspective that is set behind the slotted area of the stage floor, inserting them into sockets or shafts in the floor, which are constructed the same as those described in the fifth discourse. To create wider scenes, two sets of shafts are provided in each
(36)   order. One placed offstage of the other as indicated by X and X in the third figure (Plate 1).

These same T-guides may be also used in mounting the lights securely, mounting them and otherwise arranging them as seen in Figure 9a: A is a plank or board four or five inches wide and as long as necessary to accommodate the lights; a hook (2) is attached at the top of the plank on the opposite side to where the lights are mounted; a ring or staple (4) is attached to the top of the T-guide into which the hook (2) is inserted when mounting the lights.

It is also important to mention that when the third or fourth order of slots is used to close off the scene of the perspective, these wings should be mounted on chariots, not T-guides, otherwise the side wings of the perspective set on T-guides will be seen owing to their height. Therefore, the wings that are used to close off the scene should be mounted on the wider chariots that are set in the same slot so that their ends abut each other. Then, as they are (37) moved onstage, they close off the scene as desired.

Tenth Discourse Relating to the Tenth Figure
On the Various Arrangements of Rigging
the Chariots to the
Drums, as Well as Axles and Tracks
(Plate 5/Plate 6)

In the above diagrams I have illustrated how all the chariots of each set of wings are operated off a single drum by means of four lines, or one line that is attached to the front edge of each chariot. In the tenth figure, diagram A (Plate 5) shows how to arrange each order with just two lines. One line is attached to the drum from the onstage and offstage chariot of each order as indicated by 1 and 2. Only these two lines are attached to the central drum. The other chariots are attached to these as indicated by 3 and 4. The same procedure works for each order.

In diagram B one sees how one can operate the chariots with only two (38) lines by using two drums. The chariots are rigged together as indicated by lines 1 and 2. And the other two are labeled 3 and 4. As indicated, one end is attached to the drum and the other to the chariot. One pulls forward and the other pulls back.[13]

[13]This explanation is not clear. The rigging as indicated in diagram B will not move the chariots on and offstage, even with two drums. The chariots will move onstage as explained, but when they are supposed to move offstage, according to the depicted rigging, chariot 1 (left) will not move as one of the ropes on chariot 2 (right) is mistied. One line must be tied to the onstage edge of the chariot to make the system work.

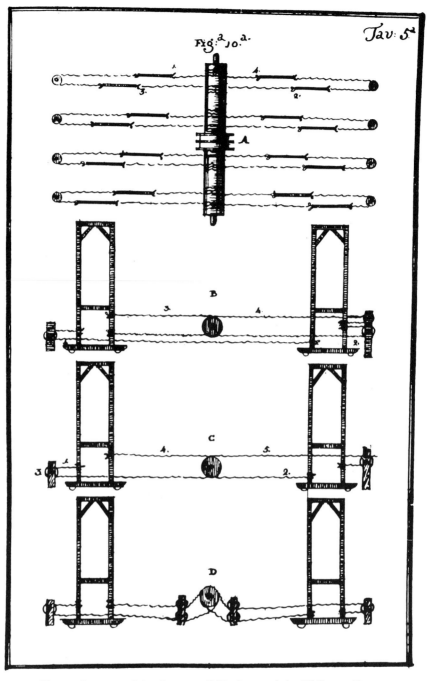

Plate 5. Courtesy of the Comune di Modena and the Biblioteca Estence.

Construction of theatres and theatrical machines

Diagram C is simpler than arrangement B, requiring less rope. After attaching the chariots together with the rope 1-2, through the pulley 3, the other line 4-5 is wrapped around the drum in such a manner that when 4 advances one chariot, 5 withdraws the other.

The chariots for carrying the *prospettiva* are put in each of the longer slots of each set and rigged to a capstan that will move them manually, as shown in diagram D. If the amount of rope indicated in D is not necessary, they can be rigged as indicated in diagram C. If, however, they are operated by only one capstan, they can be very difficult to move onstage or off, especially when mounted with the *prospettiva*. Therefore, they can be rigged as shown in diagram E. That is, each chariot is rigged with its individual capstan situ- (39) ated on each side that is operated by a single man. One man for each capstan ensures a faster shift, much easier to operate than the four-man operation necessary for the arrangement in diagram D. The only problem with the individual capstans, which does not occur with the one capstan, such as indicated in diagrams C and D, is to make them all move in unison, since they do move separately. When the single central drum is used, they will always move in unison but very slowly because of the great weight of all the wings. In this case the handles of the capstans at each end of the drum must be long enough so that two men can grasp each arm, and in this case it works best when the drum is centered between the chariots.

The arrangement in diagram F (Plate 6) utilizes a single capstan, using wooden arms. The chariots arranged in this order require little manpower to move them, but they move very slowly. However, this arrangement can be used for *prospettiva* or other things which should open or close slowly.

The drawing G diagrams an arrangement of two chariots operated by a horizontal windlass that advances one wing while withdrawing the other si- (40) multaneously as the windlass is turned.

The diagram H indicates another method of manually opening and closing the *prospecttiva*. It rolls on the stage floor and the wings open and close in the following manner. Let the dotted line 6-7 indicate the stage floor upon which the wings 8 and 9 roll. A beam 1-2 is set above the *prospettiva* at the height of the wings to which pulleys are attached at 3, 4, 5. Four more pulleys are attached to the top corners of the wings, as indicated at 10, 11, 12, 13. Then, a thin rope, fastened to wing 8 at the point 14, is threaded through the pulleys 10, 3, 4, and 12, and fastened to the other wing at point 15. The process is repeated on the other wing in reverse, that is, the rope is attached to wing 9 at point 16, and threaded through pulleys 13, 5, 4, and 11, and fastened

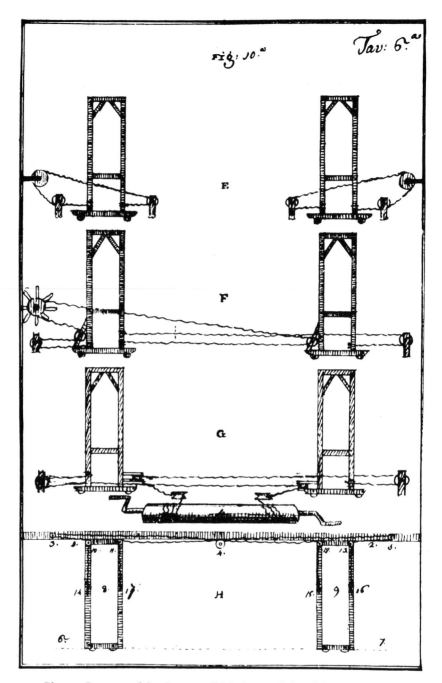

Plate 6. Courtesy of the Comune di Modena and the Biblioteca Estence.

to wing 8 and point 17. When the ropes have been so arranged, it follows that when wing 8, for example, is advanced onstage, wing 9 will advance at the same time. The same is true when they are withdrawn offstage.

Be advised that all rigging of the ropes to the chariots and pulleys is done behind the wings. For better understanding, I have shown them in front.   (41)

Eleventh Discourse on the Eleventh Figure
Another Invention for Operating the
Chariots during a Scene Change
(Plate 7)

1 and 2 represent two orders of chariots connected from the rear with ropes threaded through the pulleys 3, as illustrated in Plate 7. Then a beam, as indicated by A, is set in place of the drum below stage, which served the purpose of the drum. Small wheels attached along the length of the beam move it through a strong smooth track. A cross section of the beam B shows its construction and assembly. The beam is of sufficient length to accommodate the whole system of orders of chariots, similar to the drum. However, the track in which the beam moves must be long enough to accommodate the movement of the beam in both directions, thus ensuring that the beam will always stay in position. Ropes, passing through the pulleys 5, are attached permanently to the beam from the onstage edges of the chariots, as illustrated at 4   (42) of the cross section B. The ropes should be rigged in such a way that when the chariots are withdrawn offstage the ropes are taut and in a straight line from the chariot to the beam. When the beam is moved, the chariots will move to their forward position. A ring 6 is attached to the ends of the beam, and to move the beam, ropes or cables attached to these are threaded through the pulleys 7 and 9, set at an appropriate distance, and attached to the winch 8. These ropes move in opposition to each other as the winch is turned. Thus, they move the beam forward and backward, causing the wings on the chariots to appear and disappear. The drawing indicates that a second winch such as 8, with another set of lines, can be added to increase the turning power, thus making the operation easier and faster.

The four lines may also be attached to the ring 6, and then rigged to a drum that is mounted horizontally below stage as is seen at D in the diagram. It has a double sheave in the center on which the two lines are rigged

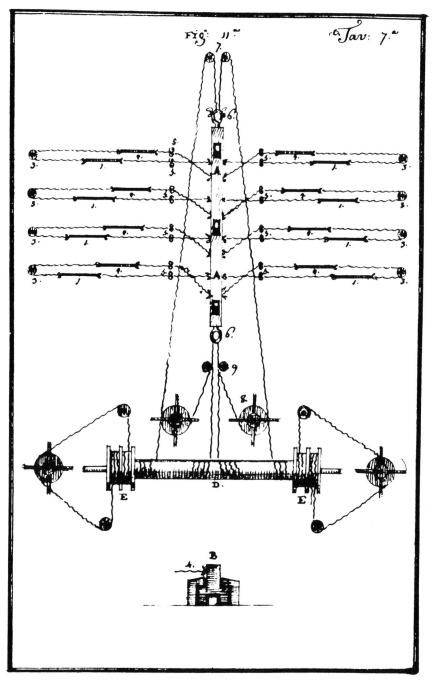

Plate 7. Courtesy of the Comune di Modena and the Biblioteca Estence.

94

around, running opposite to each other. However, it is better to use a double sheave at each end of the drum, which is connected to a separate winch, as indicated at E. The movement will be quicker because it is always easier to apply power when the men are separated and can move faster. (43)

The method that uses the double winches instead of a drum is very good because the shift moves rapidly. The men who work the winches do not have to take great care to stay out of each other's way, as they do not have to move as much.

This invention is a little capricious, although not too much so, for use in especially large stages where, because of the friction of the ropes through the pulleys 5, a great deal of force is required to move the beam.

Twelfth Discourse on the Twelfth and Thirteenth Figures
The Arrangement of Things Necessary
for Aerial Operations
(Plate 8)

Having explained the construction of the stage, the chariots and their opera-tion, I shall now explain the principles for aerial operation. I shall explain first the arrangement of the most important parts and what is necessary for their operation. (44)

Most necessary are the catwalks that allow the stagehands to move about above stage. Next are the double tracks or aerial slots that extend across the stage for the machines, and they are positioned directly above the streets of the stage below. When not in use for the machines, they can be used as crossover catwalks. Next, the platforms that are necessary for the various ma-chines, and then whatever else is necessary.

Above all, the most convenient are the tracks that run laterally from back to front of the stagehouse for the movement of aerial effects toward the audi-ence. It is true that however useful they may be, they are seldom used be-cause I believe they complicate the hanging of sky-borders, ceiling pieces, and other items.

The lateral catwalks do not permit the permanent hanging of sky-borders, or even raising and lowering them when desirable. The same is true in regard to ceiling pieces. The great usefulness of these catwalks has led me to invent a (45)

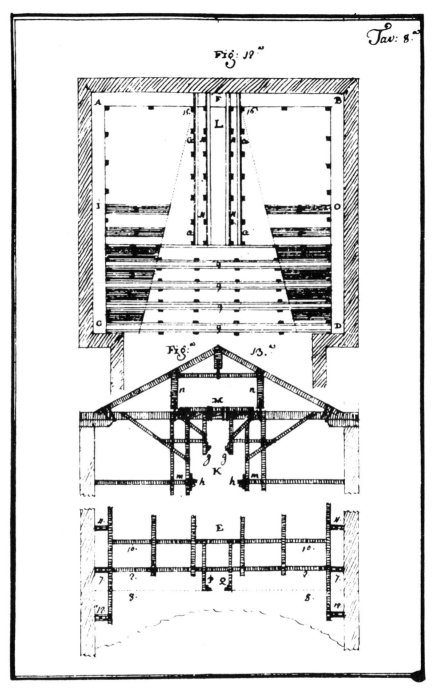

Plate 8. Courtesy of the Comune di Modena and the Biblioteca Estence.

method of raising sky-borders, ceilings, wings, etc., that will not be impeded by the catwalks, which are most useful on all stages regardless of size.

For example, let AVCD of diagram L, in Figure 12, represent the stage and the sets of slots in the stage floor 3. First, the principal catwalks, indicated as CIA, AFB, and BOD, are 4 feet wide. These are set 30 inches above the top edge of the first sky-border, as indicated in the front elevation drawing E in the thirteenth figure in which the catwalk is labeled 7 and the top edge [dotted line] of the border 8.

The main stairway to these catwalks is located at A on the stage floor and the stairway to the substage area at B. These should be as commodious as possible, since they are used continuously during the operations.

At the height of the aforementioned catwalks, the tracks that extend across   (46) the stage are suspended directly above the streets between the sets of slots in the stage floor, as indicated by 2 in diagram E. One must be careful that the overall width of these tracks and their supporting tie beams do not protrude into the air space above the chariot slots below, and the rear edge of the rear track is 6 feet 12 inches forward of the chariots' air space, as indicated by the four sets, labeled 9 in diagram L. This space is needed when sky-borders are hung from the aerial slots. When sky-borders are desired behind these, the space between the front track of the aerial slots and the rear slot of each set of chariot slots is left clear.

When not in use the tracks of these aerial slots serve as a crossover walkway to carry things from one side of the stagehouse to the other, as the space between the tracks is trapped with boards that are hinged to the outside edge of the tracks so that they can be raised up out of the way when the tracks are used for some cart or machine.

Another set of tracks, identical to the first, is set between 4 and 5 feet above   (47) the first, high enough so the movements of the cart or machines moving in the lower track will not be impeded. These tracks are fastened to the same tie beams that support the first, as indicated by 10 in diagram E. However, these upper tracks remain open and are not used as crossover runways.

The tie beams that support these tracks are suspended perpendicular from the rafters above, joined, and firmly attached on both sides, in accordance with the practices of good carpentry, so they will not sway or bow out when carts and machines move through them. Also, they should be suspended, so they will not obstruct the borders in the air space above the streets.

Beneath the main catwalks, A, I, C and B, O, D, at least the length of the slotted area of the stage floor I-C and O-D, another catwalk is hung suffi-

(48)   ciently lower so that one can walk freely, yet high enough above the stage floor so that the wings can move freely without bumping into them. These catwalks are very convenient for operating machinery as well as providing storage space for machinery when necessary.

Similarly, another catwalk, as indicated by 11 and 12 in diagram E, built above the main catwalk is very useful, especially for the operation of the heavier equipment, where all possible conveniences are advantageous.

The stairways connecting these catwalks should be conveniently located, but not where they become obstructions.

The tracks that run forward above the stage are indicated as g and h in diagram L, in the twelfth figure. They are of two sizes, one wider than the other. The narrower one is arranged above the wider, as seen in diagram K of the thirteenth figure. As is plainly seen in the cross section, they are suspended from the rafter studs. The narrower one marked g is placed above the wider one marked h. The wider tracks, marked h, are created for the large

(49)   machines and its width depends upon the size of the stagehouse. However, the width of the lower track is not more than the distance between the last set of side wings immediately in front of the *prospettiva*.

The narrow track is half as wide as the lower one, more or less, according to the accommodations of the stagehouse, and according to the type of machinery to be used.

The narrow track is suspended from the supporting truss beam M, with tie beams low enough in order that the carts of the machines can travel freely, as is indicated in diagram K. In the same manner, the distance between tracks g and h must be of sufficient height to allow the car to pass through freely.

The tracks must be joined firmly and braced solidly, so they will be strong enough to resist and support the heavy weight and firm enough to neither spread nor move. Great care must be taken in all these matters.

(50)   A catwalk built along the outside edges of the wide track, as indicated by m in diagram K, will allow someone to attend the machines during their operation in case an accident should occur.

The closer the tracks are extended toward the audience the better it is for the large machines. However, in my diagram I have extended them only as far forward as the fourth order of slots, as seen in Figure 12.

Flooring is laid over the banks of rafters, which extend the length of the stagehouse, at least the width (M) between the support beams (N). This floor space is very useful for rigging winches, capstans, and other machinery.

Other platforms can be suspended from above whenever they are needed for the various operations for sky-borders, ceiling pieces, or other machinery. But I have not given any instructions on their construction.

It only remains to point out that there is so much timber and so much weight in this stagehouse construction that great care should be taken in the selection of the timbers as well as in the construction. (51)

The aforementioned tracks g and h should be constructed of hard wood such as walnut, because if they are made of soft wood the large wheels of the carts will cut into them. In addition, the timbers of these tracks must be very thick, not only to support the weight of the machines but also to ensure that they will always traverse them without fear or danger of them falling off.

Discourse Thirteen on the Fourteenth Figure
On the Arrangement of Skies and Ceilings I
(Plate 9)

Having arranged the catwalks, tracks, and all as I have explained, it is necessary to discuss the arrangements of the skies and ceilings. The variety of skies that I use in the operations, including the serene, tempestuous, starry, and luminous, as well as a variety of ceilings, are all necessary for the many changes I make. The quantity and size of these borders can create havoc for the other aerial operations; nevertheless, the way I arranged these things make these problems impossible.

First of all, these skies can be made stationary or movable, and by movable I mean they can be raised or lowered. By skies I mean the sky-borders that are used most often in scenes where there are no ceilings, since the tem- (52) pestuous or starry skies, or any other, are needed only for special scenes.

They must be grouped together in their frames so that each border is separated from the other and runs straight. Since one conceals the other, it is necessary that one rises as the other descends. When a group of borders is set behind the ceiling pieces, it is possible that they can be stationary. I shall illustrate both methods.

When I talk about the arrangement of these sky-borders and ceilings, I mean only those units that are hung in front of the lateral track labeled g and h in Figure 12 (Plate 8). However, regardless of the size of these pieces,

99

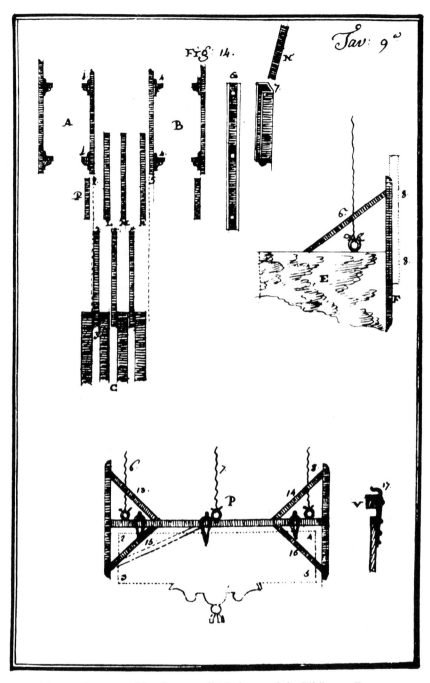

Plate 9. Courtesy of the Comune di Modena and the Biblioteca Estence.

whether sky-borders or ceiling pieces, they can be arranged in a variety of ways to allow them to pass each other. However, some sort of controlling mechanism is necessary on each end to hold them plumb as they move up and down and to keep them from flapping or fluttering when in motion. (53)

It is possible to do this in several ways, and as I have used many, I shall describe the method I found to be the best. They are arranged between the tracks that are placed above the streets on the stage floor, Plate 9. The tie beam 2 of track I is plumb with the upstage side of slot number 3. The same amount of space, as I mentioned in the previous discourse, that separates the individual slots is left between the beam 5 and the foremost slot of each order. In the space between the tie beams 2 and 5, an arrangement of three tracks are set. These are built as part of the stagehouse over every street of the stage floor. They may be called border tracks to distinguish them from other tracks or slots, since they are, in effect, open channels as indicated by D. They are arranged in pairs, set as far off to the sides of the stagehouse as is necessary to accommodate the widths of the sky-borders and ceiling pieces. The border frames E slide through the channel 8, and the end rails of this frame F extend above the frame far enough so that when the border is lowered the upper end of the rail F remains in the channel. The end rail F is reinforced with the diagonal brace 6, as illustrated, and the running edge as (54) well as the ends of this rail is rounded off so it will slide along in the channel easily without fear of catching on anything. And to make them move even easier, thin iron channels (G) may be inserted in these wooden channels, thus ensuring the borders will move up and down unhindered and always remain in trim.

These channels are long enough so that the frames of the sky-borders and ceiling pieces are always engaged when they are at their highest or lowest point. Care should be taken that the channels do not extend beyond the bottom edge of the borders in their lowest position. The best arrangement is illustrated in drawing E where the channel indicated by the dotted line 8 extends down only a portion over the end rail. This arrangement will conceal the channel from the audience on the auditorium floor even when the frames are raised.

The first set of channels facing the audience H are used for the sky- (55) borders, as they are most often used and they hang directly in front of the first order of chariot wings. The other two sets may be used for ceiling pieces or other sky-borders, depending on what is needed. And these are hung so that borders L and M will move beyond the chariot wings 9, 10, and 11. Thus, the border M is the horizontal complement to the perpendicular sliding wings 11, and the same is true with L and 10. As I have already mentioned, chariot 9 is only used for individual pieces.

The borders are arranged so that they come in behind the wings and not flush above them. To bring them in to join exactly together, as they should appear, is impossible, as the operation is so quick and they would not come together on cue simultaneously. And if the borders come in first, the wings cannot advance onstage enough, as they would jam up on the borders, causing great consternation. Thus, to prevent such a mishap, the borders should fly in behind the wings.

(56)   The sky-borders and ceiling pieces are set in channel tracks to keep them plumb as they are raised and lowered. Consequently, there is no need to worry about them jaming one another, since they are plumb and hanging as border H shows. This absolutely must be done. These frames will always warp in the center due to their width, even if they are reinforced with braces, and due to this curvature they can easily jam.

Setting the borders in the channel tracks is only desirable in operations where the first border is a sky-border, as has been mentioned, and the other two are used for ceilings or different skies. In order to have the operations of these borders work well, I think it wise to use wooden frames as illustrated in diagram P, at least for the last two units of the border. These work as border chariots, which we called "hidden chariots." The actual border units are hung on these border chariots just as wings are hung on the chariot guides, and they are arranged and changed overhead, as it is easy to attach and detach them to and from the border chariots, which are interchangeable in the channel tracks.

(57)   This border chariot P can be made of a joined beam and braces 13 and 14. However, the two lower braces are made of single boards of poplar wood notch jointed to the back of the crossbeam in such a way as not to add to the thickness of the frame.

The longer the lower braces are, 15 and 16, the more support they will provide for the chariot, as the dotted line of brace 15 indicates, strengthening it as shown.

The border chariots will be wider than the sky-border so that it will track well in the channel tracks, as indicated in diagram P, where the sky-border is indicated by dotted lines between 2, 3, 4, 5. One need not worry about the frame cutting into the tracks. This border chariot is rigged and suspended with at least three sets of lines, as indicated by 6, 7, 8 in the same diagram.

The border is attached to the border chariot and being framed it does not stretch wider when attached to the chariot. It can be attached in several ways, but of all of these, I have decided the following way is the best, as is illustrated in diagram V. Three iron hooks (17) are securely fastened to the beam of the border chariot and the border proper is tied to these hooks with ropes, being careful that the ropes are all trimmed to the same length so that the border will hang even at its proper height when attached. The end of the border proper can be attached to the braces of the border chariot with a hook-and-eye arrangement.

(58)

Fourteenth Discourse on the Fifteenth Figure
On the Arrangement of Ceilings and Skies II
(Plate 10)

I have explained how to construct the border chariots for the skies and ceilings, and how to operate and how to attach this sky-border to them. It remains to explain their rigging which is as follows:

The border chariots are rigged in the same way as those for the stage, with a drum and its double sheave, running the length of the stagehouse, that is, the first two chariots of an order operated by one drum and the third one by another.

The two front border chariots are rigged as illustrated in diagram O in the fifteenth figure. To raise the sky-border, the first ceiling piece is lowered. By this I mean that the lines of the first ceiling are rigged on the drum to turn in the opposite direction as do those that turn the sky-border, as the design clearly shows. The two lines moving opposite to each other are rigged from the double sheave to the winch where they are rigged in the same fashion, making sure that there are sufficient turns around the sheaves so each may run its course; thus, when the sky piece is raised, the ceiling border is lowered into its position.

(59)

Thus, the rigging of these two orders of border chariots is as I have diagramed it. Little force or pressure is needed to turn the winch to make them move, as the one border counterweights the other. I will not go into further detail, as the diagram is perfectly clear. I shall only indicate that the drum is

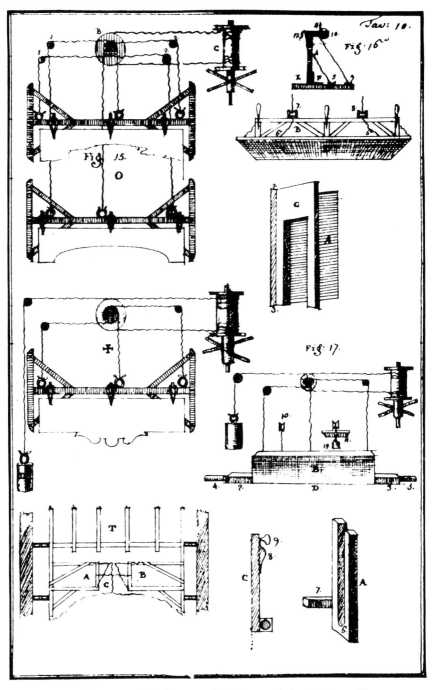

Plate 10. Courtesy of the Comune di Modena and the Biblioteca Estence.

labeled A, the double sheaves B, and the capstan or winch E. The pulleys (2) are set plumb with the rigging of the lines so they run directly to the chariots from the drum.

The last border chariot I rig to a separate drum and sheave, as illustrated in diagram ✢ of the fifteenth figure. To raise it without having to exert a great deal of pressure on the winch, I rigged a counterweight to the sheave, equal to the weight of the border chariot. The sheave must be strong enough to carry the weight. Thus it will turn quickly with little effort.

Fifteenth Discourse on Diagram T of the Fifteenth Figure (60)
How to Make Stationary Skies
(Plate 10)

When stationary skies are necessary, they are hung behind the chariot borders in the space behind the last order of wings, as indicated by 9 in Figure 14. They are arranged like those behind the guide chariots with enough open space between so that they can move as indicated between 5 and 11 (Plate 9).

Stationary wings can also be hung without leaving any space between the channel tracks and the chariot borders. This is expedient when the tracks are very narrow, hanging them beneath the tracks, as indicated by the border P beneath track 2 in the fourteenth figure (Plate 9), where it will not be in the way. The sky-border, using the wooden framework T-A-B indicated in diagram T of the fifteenth figure (Plate 10), is secured to the side catwalks and/or to the track tie beams, as indicated in diagram E of the thirteenth figure (Plate 9). It is constructed with an opening in the center or some other part, as it sometimes happens that the machines must somehow move forward toward the audience. It is solid and strong, as indicated by C. The width of the opening in these borders is determined by the width of whatever must pass through.

The flaps to close the opening between the frames A and B are reinforced (61) in the rear by whalebone staves that are sewn to the back of the flaps to keep the cloth ridged when they open close, flaps indicated by the wavy lines at C. When the machines on copper cables, channels, or anything else move through these borders, these flaps give way and then flap back into place. The wooden framework is covered with canvas to represent the sky.

There are many ways to make the machines that pass through these openings, but at the moment I am only talking about those that move the length of the stagehouse in their tracks, in order to explain how they are rigged beneath. These tracks are situated just above the sky-borders, as indicated in diagram E of the thirteenth figure by letters P and Q. Then the cart is arranged in these tracks as necessary. These tracks should be constructed so that they can be attached temporarily to the connecting tie beams, and removable so they won't interfere with the operations of the lateral tracks over which they cross. And they should be free of any obstructions.

(62)   Whatever methods are necessary and convenient, the best suited and most workable for the operation are used to raise and reset these longitudinal tracks.

Sixteenth Discourse on the Sixteenth Figure
How to Represent Chambers
or Closed Rooms
(Plate 10)

To vary the effect and please the audience, chambers or rooms, which give the effect of being enclosed with walls and ceilings, are very often represented. The stage wings are adapted for the walls according to the necessities for practical opening, such as windows through which other apartments can be seen.

(63)   This type of setting uses both the side wings and the ceiling borders, which are joined together. The side wings are double wings, as indicated by A in the sixteenth figure. The wing A is attached to the chariot and the wing C is swung open by hand to "close the setting." A is seen through the doorway of C, which can represent another room. These make excellent scenes but they are difficult to light, especially when they are all aligned to form walls in which there are no openings or "breaks," such as figures, columns, statues, etc. These kinds of "breaks" are necessary for lighting, as indicated by sections 2 and 3 of diagram C in Figure 16. Aside from the beauty they add to the setting, and the aforementioned advantage for lighting, they also conceal the lashing and the edges of which are never joined perfectly.

When the open wing C does not have practical doors or windows, it is not (64) necessary to cover wing A with cloth, as it will not be visible.

The ceiling borders consist of double frames, as indicated by B and D. Frame B is not covered with cloth and is attached to the border chariot. D falls down to form the flat ceiling when it is lowered into position.

The ceiling borders that are lowered to form the flat ceiling may be constructed in various ways. One that I have utilized has no rigging and is operated by hand; it is an easy, quick, and quite trouble-free operation that can be synchronized with the other operations when it is lowered and raised.

Flats D and B are hinged together, as indicated at F in the side view drawing, and the edge E of flat D joins the next ceiling section. They are wide enough to extend over the side wings and to align themselves easily with the ceiling pieces. The fall of the hinged flat is controlled by the ropes shown at 4 (65) and 5, which prevents the flat D from falling too far. One or two additional dead-tie lines can be added for better control.

To lower and raise the ceiling piece, two ropes are attached to the hinged piece at 6, which are threaded through the pulleys 7 and 8 that are fastened to the top edge of frame B. To operate, loosen the ropes and the hinged flat will fall backward. To close, pull the ropes 11 that are attached to frame D at 9 up through pulley 10 and tie off on hook 12, which is attached to the top ends of frame B.

When this method is used to create this kind of ceiling, the ceiling frames can be removed easily from the border chariots that can then in turn be used for other operations, which cannot be done if the ceiling pieces are raised and lowered by rigging them to a drum. And for this operation, specially assigned men under a good supervisor are a necessity.

Seventeenth Discourse on the Seventeenth Figure
Another Demonstration and Rules for (66) Arranging Flat Ceilings
(Plate 10)

Even though it is simple and effective, the aforementioned method for this type of ceiling may be objected to because of the great strain on the lines caused by the weight of the double frames. Consequently, I wish to explain another invention for lowering ceiling pieces to a horizontal plane and raising them, using the same rigging. It is very practical because it does not use the border chariots but simply the ceiling piece itself. It runs in vertical tracks but of a different nature than any that I have previously mentioned.

The tracks are open the entire length except at the bottom where they are capped with the cleat as indicated by 6 in diagram A of the seventeenth figure. A batten is fastened to the rear of the bottom edge of border B, as numerals 2 and 3 indicate, extending beyond the edges as far as is necessary, depending on the width of the border, and dowels are inserted into the ends

(67) of this batten, as indicated by numerals 4 and 5. These dowels run up and down in track A. The batten itself strengthens the border and helps guide it in the tracks.

Having constructed the border as described, it is rigged to a drum, as diagramed in figure x of the fifteenth figure (Plate 9). When the border is lowered, the dowels 4 and 5, moving down the track A, will be stopped when they hit the cleat 6. The border continues to fall backward to lower itself to the horizontal plane of the front edge, which remains at the level of the cleat 6. In rigging this ceiling piece to the drum, only enough rope is necessary to allow the piece to fall into place. As the lines also serve to hold the flat taut in position, any superfluous length would allow the flat to droop downward.

Since it is possible that the ceiling piece fall forward rather than back, small cleats of wood are attached to the outside edges of the tracks, as indicated by 7 on track A. They are set at equal heights on both tracks and are of sufficient length to ensure that the borders will not trip forward. Then, on the rear of the side edges of the ceiling frame, a curved piece of wood shaped as indicated by 8 on the profile diagram of border C is nailed to the frame. As the border falls down the groove A, the cleat on the border 8 will trip over the cleat 7 on the track, forcing the frame to fall backward and into place as it

(68) should. The number 9 on C indicates iron eyelets to which lines can be attached when the ceiling pieces are removed out of the tracks and replaced by other types that are rigged in the same way; however, they may be used.

In this invention there is a special line attached to the center of the free edge of the ceiling piece that holds it taut and prevents it from sagging. Two more lines are attached to the iron eyelets 9 of D and then threaded through the pulleys 10 and then dropped through a hole in the catwalk and attached

(69) to a weight below 12. This weight is just heavy enough to keep the lines taut and to haul it out when the ceiling piece is to be raised. The ropes are just

long enough that when the ceilings are down, the underside of the catwalk will serve as a stop cleat for the counterweight, thus holding the ceiling piece level. Then when the ceilings are raised, the weight will descend. However, these pulleys and planks must be just high enough and at the correct level so that they can be effective as the counterweight runs its course and, yet, not be visible from the audience when the ceiling pieces are raised.

Eighteenth Discourse on the Eighteenth Figure

On the Arrangement of the Skies and Ceilings When They Are Used with the Tracks That Traverse the Sides of the Stage

(Plate 11)

The sky- and ceiling-border units that are used with the tracks perpendicular to the front of the stage (g and h in Figure 13, Plate 9) are assembled in pairs for each set. This means that each border is made in two parts and that each part will be arranged as illustrated in diagram A of the eighteenth figure. First, I shall speak of the skies that in this position move onstage from the sides. Below each side of the lower perpendicular track (E) a pair of borders (70 are set in tracks, as indicated in the side view, drawing B, arranged with just enough width to allow the border chariot to move easily within, on the wheels attached as shown. Wheel 1 runs on track 3 and wheel 2 runs on track 4, or as indicated by the wheels 5 and 6 that carry the border C (in diagram A) along the traveler track 7. Side rails are unnecessary for these tracks, as they are supported sufficiently by the tie beams suspended from above. These traveler tracks carry the border C on the wheels 5 and 6 in diagram A. The onstage edge of each border is fitted with whalebone staves that extend and support the canvas end of the border, as indicated by D, for the same reasons as explained in the fifteenth discourse. Wheel 5 is so positioned that when it reaches the onstage edge of track 7, the onstage edge of the border (8) will join the onstage edge of an identical border moving onstage from the op- (71) posite side of the stage. The border is rigged with lines to a small drum (F) that moves the border frame on or offstage, as diagramed, tying the one end of the line to the border frame below wheel 5, then threading it through

109

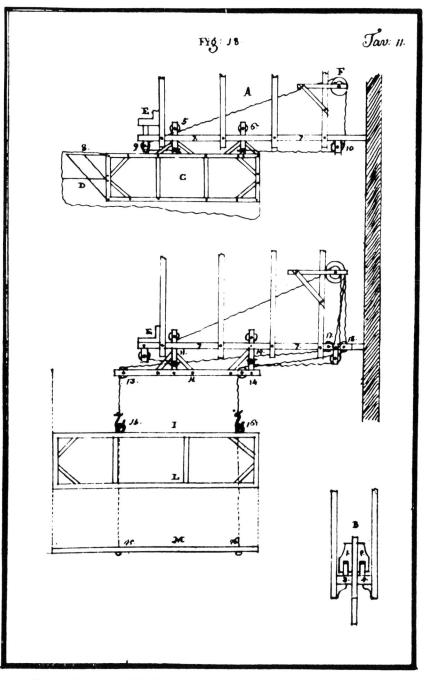

Plate 11. Courtesy of the Comune di Modena and the Biblioteca Estence.

pulley 9 onto the drum F, where it is wrapped around the drum a few turns and then threaded through pulley 10 and tied off on the border frame below pulley 6. This arrangement moves the borders easily, and the drum should be placed so it will not become an obstruction on the crossover walkways.

When all the borders have been so arranged in pairs, each set of borders, from the rear forward, are withdrawn offstage as the large machine travels forward on the track perpendicular to them, and then they close immediately as the machine passes through the opening. This effect is very beautiful to see when the movements are all timed and coordinated.

The arrangement is identical for the ceiling borders as illustrated in diagram O. The only difference is that for the greater convenience the traveler tracks (7) are set right under the longitudinal track E. When this is the case, the skies and ceilings will hang very high, so the traveler wheels are not attached directly to the border frame but to the beam (M) that is fitted with (72) pulley wheels 13 and 14, which allow the border frame to be lowered and raised as it moves on and offstage. A set of lines is rigged to a larger drum than used in the previous operation, that is, the lines 15 and 16 hooked to the top of the frame I are then threaded through pulleys 13 and 14 and then through pulleys 17 and 18 and up to the drum.

With this kind of rigging, it is possible to hang many kinds of borders in this fashion, and it is very convenient for raising borders and hooking and unhooking them as desired.

Some scenes are not as deep and in this case the sets and the amount of scenery necessary are curtailed. However, when borders are not used in the setting, a cloth drop is hung directly behind the *prospettiva* to mask the top of the scenes.

This operation is performed with the same machinery as indicated in diagram O.

In this case the chariot H carries the border frame as far onstage as indi- (73) cated by the dotted line on the left side of the diagram, which indicates the center of the stage. The cloth is attached to the face of the frame in front of the chariot. It is as long and wide as is necessary. A batten is fastened to the bottom edge of the cloth, as indicated by M, and this batten is rigged with two ropes, as indicated by 25 and 26, that are threaded through pulleys 13 and 14 and 17 and 18 and wound around a large drum. When the ropes are drawn up, the bottom batten should abut the frame so that the cloth is held straight and tight in order that the chariot can be moved offstage without fouling the cloth.

III

(74)   Although these cloths hang behind the *prospettiva,* as described, the invention I have just described may be used behind any set of wings. However, when the tracks run the entire length of the stage, a closing may be achieved by yet another way. The drop is attached to a roller batten, of sufficient size to carry the cloth, and this roller batten is suspended beneath a track that spans the stage from side to side. A pulley wheel is attached to one end of this batten and a rope is rigged around the pulley wheel, which is used to raise and lower the drop. An iron counterweight is attached to the rope to stabilize the movement of the drop at any height. These machines should only be used when they move easily and do not cause any problems. I have not provided a diagram, as the operation is easily understood from the description.

(75)
Nineteenth Discourse on the Nineteenth Figure
Another Method of Changing Scenes
Which is Easy and Convenient Particularly
for Stages with Little Offstage Space
(Plate 12)

The worst defect of a stagehouse is not to have sufficient backstage space to move about freely during the operations of shifting scenery, which makes it almost impossible to work efficiently.

Therefore, in order to work on this kind of stage, the shifting of scenery must be accomplished in a different manner than I have explained so far. Although chariots are still used, they do not come into view from the sides of the stage but they appear from below. And to do this the stage must be constructed differently, eliminating the last slot, which is used to close the *prospettiva* or bring onstage individual set pieces, from all orders except the

(76)   last two, as indicated in the ground plan A of Figure 19. This diagram represents one-half of the stage floor, but its arrangement is completely different from what I have previously shown. All the slots are 8 inches wide with 6 inches between when used in connection with borders; when not, the slots need to be only 3 inches wide with only 3 inches between.

The substage area is constructed as the side elevation drawing D illus-

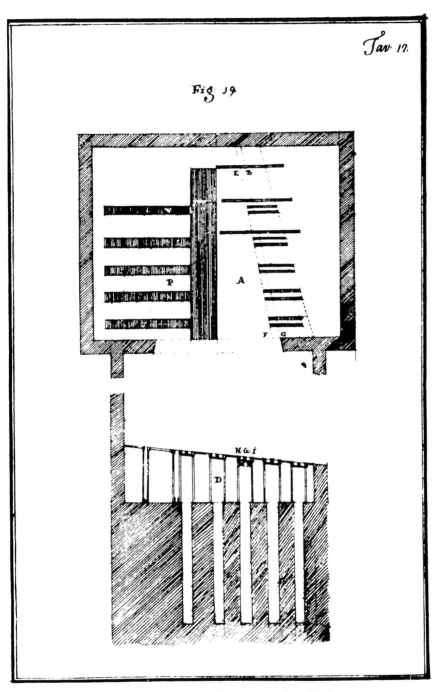

Plate 12. Courtesy of the Comune di Modena and the Biblioteca Estence.

trates. Access areas at least 30 inches wide must be left on all sides of the sets of wings, and the slot pits must be deep enough to accommodate easily the wings for the scenes, as the wings will always be mounted or dismounted from the chariots on the floor of the substage level.

The chariots for the long slots, which are used to close the scene, are operated as in the previously mentioned system, with the wings attached and dismounted to the chariot guides on the stage floor, where some working room remains when the side wings are handled on the substage area.

(77)   A large working area should be allotted to the center of the substage area, as indicated in plan P, for the easy handling of the wings, but the slot pits should extend onstage as far as necessary to allow passage for the support of the wings.

The stage floor between the slots is a series of traps, which can be opened to lower the wings into the substage area or to remove them to a better storage area.

These traps should not be attached with hinges, as I have described earlier, because when the wings are below they will not open or close. Rather, they should be attached to the main joists of the stage floor and secured by some kind of chain. If hinges are desired, however, they must be fastened on the

(78)   top, which will not create any problems, as they are only used, as I have said, for lowering and removing wings.

The remaining area of the stage floor may be trapped with hinges from below, as we have explained in the third discourse. These traps run the width and length of the stage, constructed and joined together in such a way that the stage floor remains very solid and strong.

The joist G between the slots of the sets of wings should not be supported by the same kind of beam arrangement as are the beams that set on the outer edges of the double slots, as indicated by H and I in diagram D. Instead, the beam G is supported by cross braces from the braces that support the beams H and I, as indicated by M and N.[14] This is necessary so the beam G can be removed when the wings are to be lowered to the substage area, and these cross braces M and N should be spaced far enough apart between the supports for H and I so that the wings can slip through the trapped areas very easily.

The distance between the sets of slots on the stage, which I presume to be 30 feet deep, should be 38 inches wide.

[14]M and N are not very clear on the diagram. They appear almost directly below H and I in the cross section of the stagehouse marked D.

Twentieth Discourse on the Twentieth Figure

On the Arrangement of the Chariots in Theatres without Sufficient Offstage Space

(Plate 13)

A *gargamo* or open channel or U-shaped beam is set into the offstage end of each slot, of sufficient length to extend from the bottom of the slot pit below (79) stage to the heavens above, as illustrated by A-B in the twentieth figure. A chariot constructed as diagram F indicates is made to run in this channel beam, moving up and down with the plank 5-6 serving as the moving guide. The wings are attached to these chariots, as already explained, below stage. Diagram D indicates the shape of these slots, with the openings for the channel beams and the chariots. These beams are set far enough offstage so that they will not be visible from the audience, and the top end of the front channel must be masked with a sky border. In addition, immediately behind the rear channel a stationary wing painted to represent the sky is placed that serves to mask the opening created offstage during the wing changes, as indicated by 1 and 2 in diagram D. Thus, the opening will always be masked, especially as the two wings meet halfway as they rise and fall during the change.

For this kind of change the chariots must be rigged to a winch or drum, similar to the system illustrated in diagram O of the fifteenth figure, so when (80) one part is lowered the other rises. There is only one rope attached to each chariot, which is fastened to an iron ring mounted on the latter, as indicated at E on chariot C. When these channel beam slots are constructed, ample space should be left both in front and back of the chariots, as represented by 3 and 4 in diagram D, so that the thickness of the wings will not cause any problems as the chariots move up and down through the slots. Two rollers can be set in the perpendicular plank of the chariot to facilitate its movement in the channel beam.

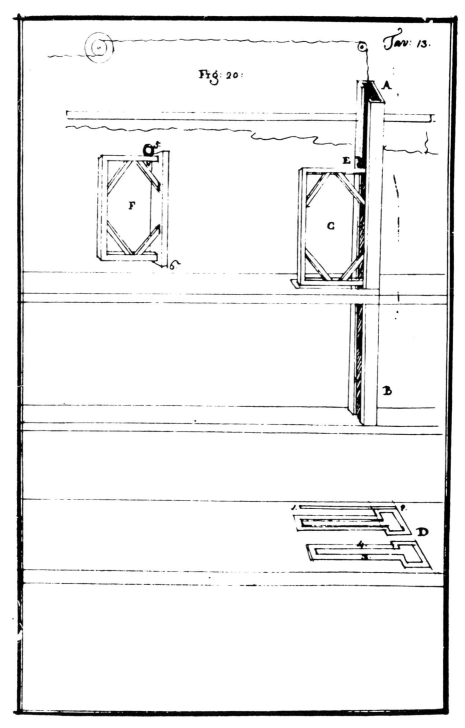

Plate 13. Courtesy of the Comune di Modena and the Biblioteca Estence.

Twenty-first Discourse on the Twenty-first Figure
On the Arrangement of Ceilings and Borders When the Stage Grooves Are Set Obliquely on the Stage Floor
(Plate 14)

When the grooves are set obliquely onstage the above arrangement is very good, but it will cause some inconvenience for the carts of the machines that run in the tracks because, since the tracks run parallel to the front of the stage, the distance the carts can move across the stage will be decreased by (81) the width of the oblique wings that obstruct the movement on both ends. It is better, however, to build them in such a way as to avoid this problem.

I have already mentioned that the smaller stages should not include in their sets of grooves a slot for the individual set pieces. In arranging the borders, however, instead of hanging them as illustrated in Figure 14 (Plate 9), the border wings themselves are hung over the slots because in such theatres two scenes with borders are enough. Besides, they can be arranged so that they can be used with a variety of side wings. In this case, the borders are hung close together, with 3 inches between the pieces, that is, between the borders C and D, as well as between the side wing N and the border O. Tracks for the machines that traverse the stage can be installed on these small stages and, even though they may be narrower than usual, this is not important, as the machines can be adapted to a smaller size, as you will eventually realize.

Twenty-Second Discourse on the Twenty-second Figure
(82)
Another Invention for Arched Borders
(Plate 14)

Although scenes with arched borders create admiration and delight the audience, the operations to change them are most difficult and taxing for those who must perform the task due to the great encumbrance they create among

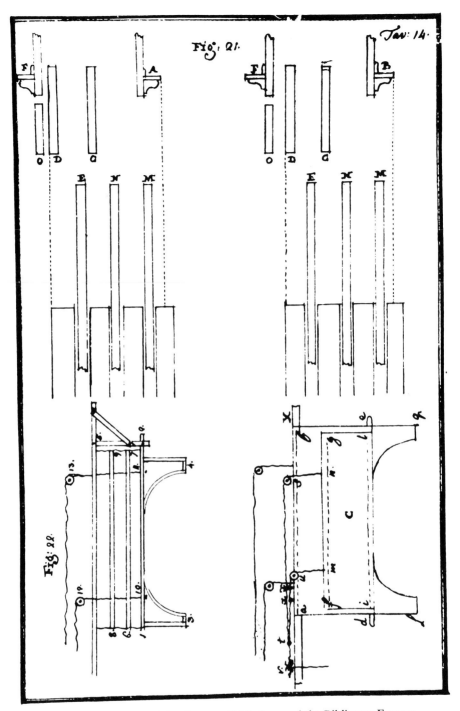

Plate 14. Courtesy of the Comune di Modena and the Biblioteca Estence.

the arches and borders in the heavens. This is especially true when the aerial machines are involved in the operation. This difficulty caused me to think of easier methods and inventions to effect these changes, not only to make the borders shift easier but to curtail their weight as well. To raise them without creating any obstacles in the fly gallery after they have worked in the scene, consider constructing them as I indicate in the present design; that is, simply make the wooden frame of the arched border one-sixth of its height, as indicated by 1, 2, 3, 4 and install it in the border grooves, as indicated at 2 and 5. These grooves are identical with those diagramed in Figure 14 (Plate 9). The ends of the bottom of the frame, as indicated by 1 and 2, extend through the grooves, as indicated by 2. In this case it will be advantageous to extend the cloth covering of the frame above the frame, so when the arched border is lowered into place it is held in place as illustrated by a and b in design C. A cloth long enough to cover the space indicated by a, d, b, e in which two or more battens, such as indicated by 6-7 and 8-9, can be attached at intervals. Then the wooden frame is rigged as is indicated, with lines 10-12 and 11-13, threading them through the battens 6-7 and 8-9. These lines are tied to the batten 1-2 at points 10 and 11, and the other ends of the lines are threaded through pulleys 12 and 13 and lead to a winch or drum. The lines are wrapped around the drum as described elsewhere. When the lines are drawn up as the border is raised, the section of the arched border from d-e of diagram C will drape itself into a double fold as a-b, rather than hang straight as will the simpler border 1, 2, 3, 4. This method of rigging was diagramed in figure O of the eighteenth figure (Plate 11).

(83)

In order for this same arch to be used as an ordinary border, another cloth can be attached to the batten d, e, which is as long as the height of the arch itself, as shown by f, i, g, l, and another batten is attached to the cloth, as indicated by f, g, in order to hold it straight and give the cloth weight. Two lines are attached to this batten, f and g at m and n, and they are threaded through pulleys u and s, which are hung off of beam X. The lines are tied together at t, and the single line is then threaded through the ring r hung on the beam X. For the best control and to keep the line in order, it is best to pass them through the eyelets x before tying them together at t. Once this is all arranged, when the line is loosened, the weight of the upper batten will cause the cloth to fall, thus covering the opening of the arch d.p.e.g., and appear as an ordinary border. The cloth d.p.e.g. is painted on one side to match the arch and the border on the other. This excellent invention should take up little space, since it cuts down the number of borders necessary as well as the space they occupy.

(84)

End of Discourses

Table of Measurements for Wing-Chariot Systems for Stagehouses of Varying Sizes

(Third Discourse of the *Costruzione*)

Motta's Ideal Layout (Figure 3 of Plate 1)

Overall depth of stagehouse: 71 feet 3 inches
Wing-chariot system occupies the front 38 feet of the stage floor
    6 orders of chariots
        3 slots to each order
        3rd slot of each order extends toward stage center
    6 orders of streets (spaces between orders of chariots)
        1st street precedes 1st order of chariots
    Streets 43 inches wide
    Slots 3 inches wide
    Spaces between slots 9 inches

Smaller Stagehouses

Overall depth of stagehouse: not more than 47 feet 6 inches
Wing-chariot system occupies front 30 feet of stage floor
    5 orders of chariots—Motta recommends 2 arrangements

1st Arrangement—A

    3 orders of 3 slots
        3rd slot of each order extends toward stage center
    2 orders of 4 slots
        3rd and 4th slots of these orders extend toward stage center
    5 orders of streets
    Streets 39½ inches wide
    Slots 3 inches wide
    Spaces between slots 8½ inches

2nd Arrangement—B

    4 orders of 3 slots
        3rd slot of each order extends toward stage center

Construction of theatres and theatrical machines

1 order of 4 slots
    3rd and 4th slots extend toward stage center
5 orders of streets
Streets 42 inches wide
Slots 3 inches wide
Spaces between slots 9 inches wide

Smallest Stagehouse

Overall depth of stagehouse: 38 feet, or less
Wing-chariot system occupied the front 27 feet of the stage floor
5 orders of chariots of either A or B arrangement, described above
5 orders of streets
    1st street 38 inches wide
    4 remaining streets 40 inches wide
    Slots 2½ inches wide
    Spaces between slots 7½ inches

Larger Stagehouse

Overall depth of stagehouse: 67 feet or more
Wing-chariot system occupies front 43 feet of stage floor
7 orders of chariots
    4 orders of 3 slots
        3rd slot extends toward stage center
    5th order of 4 slots
        3rd and 4th slots extend toward stage center
    6th order of 3 slots
        3rd slot extends toward stage center
    7th order of slots
        3rd and 4th slots extend toward stage center
7 orders of streets
Streets 45 inches wide
Slots 3 inches wide
Spaces between slots of the first 4 orders: 8½ inches
Spaces between slots of the last 3 orders: 9½ inches
Note: In all layouts the street areas behind the first two orders of chariots are
    trapped.

Stagehouse utilizing vertical moving wings because of the lack of any offstage pace (discourses 19 and 20, Plates 12 and 13)

Overall depth of stagehouse: less than 31 feet 6 inches

Wing-chariots system occupied 25 feet 3 inches of the front of stage floor

5 orders of wing chariots

    3 orders of 2 slots (for wings that move up and down)

    2 orders of 3 slots

        3rd slot extends toward stage center

    1 long slot extending toward stage center behind the

        5 orders of slots

6 orders of streets

    1st street 29 inches wide

    5 orders of streets 38 inches wide

Slots 3 inches wide

Spaces between slots 7½ inches wide

"The following are two *Oncie* of Mantova"
This drawing of "two *Oncie* of Mantova"—three inches—illustrates the dimension
Motta prescribes for the width of the slots in his wing-chariot systems. From Lodovico
Perini, *Trattato della pratica Geometri in cui oltre i principi di essa vi sono molto insegnia-
menti intorno alle varie misure, &c.* (Verona, 1727). Courtesy of Edward A. Craig.

Le seguenti sono Oncie due di Mantova.

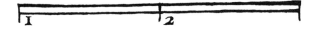

Index

Index

Orville K. Larson, an internationally known theatre historian, is Professor Emeritus of Theatre at Kent State University. His articles on Italian scenography and American scene design have appeared in national and international periodicals of theatre and art for the past thirty years. His *Stage Design for Stage and Screen* is a collection of essays on the aesthetics of American scene design.